THE KINDNESS OF OTHERS

PREVIOUSLY PUBLISHED BY THE

Lama Yeshe Wisdom Archive

Becoming Your Own Therapist, by Lama Yeshe
Advice for Monks and Nuns, by Lama Yeshe and Lama Zopa Rinpoche
Virtue and Reality, by Lama Zopa Rinpoche
Make Your Mind an Ocean, by Lama Yeshe
Teachings from the Vajrasattva Retreat, by Lama Zopa Rinpoche
Daily Purification: A Short Vajrasattva Practice, by Lama Zopa Rinpoche
The Essence of Tibetan Buddhism, by Lama Yeshe
Making Life Meaningful, by Lama Zopa Rinpoche
Teachings from the Mani Retreat, by Lama Zopa Rinpoche
The Direct and Unmistaken Method, by Lama Zopa Rinpoche
The Yoga of Offering Food, by Lama Zopa Rinpoche
The Peaceful Stillness of the Silent Mind, by Lama Yeshe
Teachings from Tibet, by various great lamas
The Joy of Compassion, by Lama Zopa Rinpoche

FOR INITIATES ONLY:
A Chat about Heruka, by Lama Zopa Rinpoche
A Chat about Yamantaka, by Lama Zopa Rinpoche

IN ASSOCIATION WITH TDL ARCHIVE, LOS ANGELES:
Mirror of Wisdom, by Geshe Tsultim Gyeltsen
Illuminating the Path to Enlightenment, by His Holiness the Dalai Lama

*May whoever sees, touches, reads, remembers, or talks or thinks about these books
never be reborn in unfortunate circumstances, receive only rebirths in situations
conducive to the perfect practice of Dharma, meet only perfectly qualified
spiritual guides, quickly develop bodhicitta and immediately
attain enlightenment for the sake of all sentient beings.*

• • • •
•

GESHE JAMPA TEGCHOK

The Kindness of Others

A COMMENTARY ON THE
SEVEN-POINT MIND TRAINING

Translated by Stephen Carlier
Edited by Andy Wistreich,
Linda Gatter and Nicholas Ribush

LAMA YESHE WISDOM ARCHIVE • BOSTON
www.LamaYeshe.com

A non-profit charitable organization for the benefit of all
sentient beings and an affiliate of the Foundation for
the Preservation of the Mahayana Tradition
www.fpmt.org

First published 2006
10,000 copies for free distribution

LAMA YESHE WISDOM ARCHIVE
PO BOX 356, WESTON, MA 02493, USA

© Geshe Jampa Tegchok 2006

ISBN 1-891868-16-0

10 9 8 7 6 5 4 3 2 1

Cover photograph by Clive Arrowsmith
Cover line art by Robert Beer
Designed by Gopa & Ted2, Inc

Please contact the LAMA YESHE WISDOM ARCHIVE
for more copies of this and our other free books

··· Contents ···

···Publisher's Acknowledgments···

WE ARE EXTREMELY GRATEFUL to our friends and supporters who have made it possible for the Lama Yeshe Wisdom Archive to both exist and function: to Lama Yeshe and Lama Zopa Rinpoche, whose kindness is impossible to repay; to Peter and Nicole Kedge and Venerable Ailsa Cameron for helping bring the Archive to its present state of development; to Venerable Roger Kunsang, Lama Zopa's tireless assistant, for his kindness and consideration; and to our sustaining supporters: Barry & Connie Hershey, Joan Halsall, Roger & Claire Ash-Wheeler, Claire Atkins, Thubten Yeshe, Doren & Mary Harper, Tom & Suzanne Castles, Richard Gere, Lily Chang Wu and Hawk Furman.

We are also deeply grateful to all those who have become members of the ARCHIVE over the past couple of years. Details of our membership program may be found at the back of this book, and if you are not a member, please do consider joining up. Due to the kindness of those who have, we now have several editors—in particular Ven. Tenzin Namdrol, Ven. Thubten Labdron and Michelle Bernard—working on our vast collection of teachings for the benefit of all. We have posted a list of our individual and corporate members on our Web site, www.LamaYeshe.com. We also thank Henry & Catherine Lau, S. S. Lim and Charmaine Wai for their help with our membership program in Singapore and Malaysia. Thank you all so much for your foresight and kindness.

In particular we thank Andy Wistreich for suggesting we publish this book and helping raise the funds required. Those who so kindly contributed include Xavi & Mena Alongina, Ros Boughtflower & Paul Wielgus, Chamtseling Buddhist Group, Dharma Friendship Foundation, Ven. Thubten Chodron, Ven. Robina Courtin, Nick Durnan, Gail Hellowell, Nick Hill, Barnaby Kent, Ven. Sangye Khadro, Kevin Middleton, Mike Miko, Reg O'Brien, Les Phillips, Richard Pope, Wendy Ridley & Steve Cragg, Saraswati Buddhist Group, Andy Wistreich & Shan Tate and several anonymous donors.

I would also like to express my gratitude for the kindness and compassion of all those other generous benefactors who have contributed funds to our work since we began publishing free books several years ago. Thankfully, you are all too numerous to mention individually in this book but we value highly each and every donation made to spreading the Dharma for the sake of the kind mother sentient beings and now pay tribute to you all on our Web site. Thank you so much.

Finally, I would like to thank the many kind people who have asked that their donations be kept anonymous; the volunteers who have given so generously of their time to help us with our mailings, especially Therese Miller; my wife, Wendy Cook, for her constant help and support; our dedicated office staff, Jennifer Barlow and Sonal Shastri; our volunteer transcribers; Veronica Kaczmarowski, Evelyn Williams, FPMT Australia & Mandala Books (Brisbane) and for much appreciated assistance with our work in Australia; and Dennis Heslop, Philip Bradley and our other friends at Wisdom Books (London) for their great help with our work in Europe.

If you, dear reader, would like to join this noble group of open-hearted altruists by contributing to the production of more free books by Lama Yeshe or Lama Zopa Rinpoche or to any other aspect of the LAMA YESHE WISDOM ARCHIVE's work, please contact us to find out how.

—Dr. Nicholas Ribush

Through the merit of having contributed to the spread of the Buddha's
teachings for the sake of all sentient beings, may our benefactors
and their families and friends have long and healthy lives,
all happiness, and may all their Dharma
wishes be instantly fulfilled.

· · · · ·

··· Editors' Introduction ···

W E ARE EXTREMELY FORTUNATE to live at a time when the
Mahayana mind training teachings abound. There was a time
not so long ago when they were much harder to find. Of course, as
many lamas point out, all of the Buddha's teachings are for training the
mind, in that mind training can be said to be the subject of the oft-
quoted verse,

Do not commit any non-virtuous actions,
Perform only virtuous actions,
Subdue your mind thoroughly—
This is the teaching of the Buddha.[1]

But in the Tibetan tradition, at least, the connotation of mind training
is the development of *bodhicitta*, the determination to attain enlightenment for the sake of all sentient beings. And of the various methods for
the development of bodhicitta, mind training emphasizes the practice
of transforming suffering into happiness, using the various problems
and obstacles we encounter in life as supports for our spiritual practice
and not allowing them to overwhelm us or even slow us down.

[1] The *Dhammapada*, Chapter 14.

Based on a couple of lines from Nagarjuna's *Precious Garland*, the main Tibetan source of the mind training teachings is Kadampa Geshe Chekawa's *Seven-Point Mind Training*. Currently there are at least fourteen English-language commentaries on this text by both Tibetan and Western teachers, as detailed in the bibliography of this book, which is another reason that we're extremely fortunate. However, the availability of these teachings is not enough. We have to put them into practice.

Therefore we are most grateful to the great Geshe Jampa Tegchok for adding his lucid explanation of how to practice mind training. With reference to a special Tibetan commentary,[2] he engages us in a debate between our inner selfish voice and our altruistic motivation, which makes this teaching especially personal in helping us take on that greatest of challenges—defeating the false logic of our own selfishness. We are honored to have been able to edit this oral teaching to make it available for worldwide distribution free of charge.

We thank Ven. Steve Carlier for his excellent translation, Ven. Geshe Lhakdor, director of the Tibetan Library of Works and Archives, Dharamsala, for allowing us to use the translation of Pabongka Rinpoche's edition of the root text found in the LTWA's *Mind Training Like the Rays of the Sun*, Clive Arrowsmith for his beautiful photography, and Jeff Cox of Snow Lion Publications for sending us Alan Wallace's teachings for reference.

[2] See Chapter 10: Conclusion.

··· 1 ···

Motivation

THE BUDDHA SAID that when we meet to teach, listen to or discuss the Dharma it is very important that we have the best possible motivation for doing so. Whether what we do is good or bad depends almost entirely on our reason for doing it—in other words, our motivation. And while this is true in general, it is especially important to have the purest possible motivation when teaching or listening to the particular thought transformation practice we are discussing here. From the side of both teacher and student a virtuous motivation is critical, otherwise they risk putting much effort into something that has no chance of a positive result.

It is extremely negative if the teacher is teaching to enhance his or her reputation, win new followers, receive many offerings or become highly venerated or the student is listening with competitive thoughts or to gain fame, a good reputation, wealth or a big following. The great Indian practitioner and scholar Atisha said that anything done merely for this life is not a Dharma practice. Moreover, while the motivations to avoid rebirth in the three lower realms or achieve complete personal liberation from cyclic existence are not negative, they are still not the best.

When your motivation for giving or listening to teachings, meditating, helping others and so forth is simply to avoid rebirth in the lower realms it is called *small scope* motivation. When it is longer term and greater than that and aimed at complete liberation from the whole of cyclic existence it is called *middle scope* motivation.

When your motivation is even greater than that and aimed at benefiting every single sentient being and if, in order to do that, you are determined to achieve the state of full enlightenment—which is completely free of all faults and has all good qualities fully developed to their highest potential—it is the supreme motivation and called that of the *great scope*. When this is your motivation, every activity in which you engage—giving, listening to or meditating on teachings and so forth—becomes a practice of the great scope and is the best and highest kind of practice you can possibly do.

What about practices associated with deities such as Medicine Buddha, Tara or Saraswati? For example, certain Medicine Buddha practices can help you overcome obstacles and illness and have a long life. Are such practices considered spiritual? It depends on your motivation.

If you genuinely feel that a long life will help you be of greater benefit to others and with that kind of attitude engage in practices for overcoming obstacles, ill health and so forth, they will definitely be spiritual because you will not be doing them merely for this life.

Engaging in such practices after you have recognized that you possess the many characteristics and supportive conditions needed for engaging in meaningful and powerful spiritual practice in this life is completely different from simply doing them for worldly purposes. A life completely free from adverse conditions that prevent such practice provides exceptional opportunities. Therefore, not only should you engage in practices that allow you to keep your life conducive to

Dharma practice but you should also abandon any urge to waste it and, instead, feel compelled to use your life to achieve enlightenment for the benefit others.

In fact, the kind of life we presently have is so exceptional that even the gods, who appear to have extraordinarily good fortune, actually have nothing like the good fortune that we do because they have no opportunity to practice Dharma.

Therefore, we should use this opportunity to pursue enlightenment for the sake of others because not only is it the very best way of using our life, it's also because all beings are basically the same as us in wanting happiness and not wanting suffering.

We all want the greatest, longest lasting and best possible happiness; we utterly dislike suffering, problems and even the slightest difficulty. That we abhor even one or two problems let alone many shows that we all want happiness and freedom from suffering, and the best way of getting what we want and avoiding that which we don't is the practice of Dharma.

We might think that even though it's important to practice Dharma, it's not essential to do so just yet because we can always do it in future lives. However, that's a very mistaken way to think because our present human life has exceptional opportunities and attributes. There are eighteen advantages to this human life—the eight freedoms and the ten richnesses—and a life like this is very difficult to find.

The perfect human rebirth is difficult to find because its causes are very difficult to create. Furthermore, it combines many different characteristics, attributes and qualities that very rarely come together and therefore there's no certainty that we'll be able to enjoy this kind of opportunity again in future. Certain things almost never happen[3] and this human life is even more difficult to acquire than those. Therefore we should definitely practice Dharma in this very life.

We might also think, "Yes, I should practice Dharma in this life but not right now—maybe next month, next year or some other time in future." This, too, is a big mistake because there's no guarantee that we'll be around that long. Our lifespan is not fixed. If we could be sure of living for, say, a hundred years, it might be reasonable to put things off for a while, but in fact our time of death is totally unfixed. We have no idea at all when we'll die. Therefore we should resolve to practice immediately.

As long as we're ignorant of such things it's quite understandable that we don't feel responsible for our future but once we do know, it's vital that we start making our life meaningful. As the Buddha taught, we are our own protector; the responsibility is ours. Nobody else can practice for us. We have to practice and take responsibility for ourselves, especially for our future lives. It's the same as when we're ill—the doctor makes the diagnosis and prescribes the appropriate medicine but it's our responsibility to actually follow the advice given and take the medicine prescribed. Nobody else can do it for us.

Over the centuries many practitioners from all four major traditions of Tibetan Buddhism have attained enlightenment in a single lifetime but it's not easy to do. It takes hard work and great intelligence. Therefore we should expect it to take many lifetimes for us to do so. But if we devote our life to developing qualities such as love and compassion and

---

[3] The teachings mention such things as stars shining at noon and rice grains thrown against a wall adhering to it. See also *Liberation in the Palm of Your Hand*, p. 319 ff.

avoid actions that harm ourselves and others as much as we possibly can there's reason to hope that in our next life we'll be able to continue from where we left off. In this way, over a series of lives, we'll gradually progress to buddhahood.

The Buddha said that all he could do was to teach the path to liberation and enlightenment and that it was then up to us whether or not we reached those states. To do so, therefore, we have to follow his advice and live according to his teachings. There's no other way. He said, "I can't pour my wisdom and compassion into your mind, wash away your negativities or remove your suffering by hand, like pulling out a thorn. All I can do is to explain what *you* have to do to achieve the freedom from suffering, realizations and qualities that I did."

Therefore, please generate the highest motivation for studying these teachings by thinking, "I must help all sentient beings as much as I possibly can. In order to do so, I must attain enlightenment. Then I will definitely be able to benefit others in the highest possible way."

Even if you don't have an extensive understanding of Buddhism, if you generate that kind of motivation you will ensure that your time is not wasted, and as you discover and read more about the Dharma, your understanding will gradually increase.

··· 2 ···

The Seven-Point Mind Training

THE SUBJECT OF THIS TEACHING is mind training [Tib: *lo-jong*],[4] which has the connotation of cleansing, or purifying, our mental, verbal and physical actions. Actually, from that point of view, all the Buddha's teachings are mind training in that they were all given for training the body, speech and mind.

The source of this teaching

This text, the *Seven-Point Mind Training*, is associated with Atisha, a great scholar and practitioner born in India in the tenth century. He received this teaching from Serlingpa, "The Man (or Teacher) from the Golden Isle," which refers to Sumatra.

There are two methods for generating and practicing bodhicitta, the sevenfold cause and effect instruction, which, during Atisha's time, was available in India, and the method of exchanging self and others, which was not. Therefore Atisha had to undertake the difficult, thirteen-month journey from India to Indonesia to receive the teachings on exchanging self and others.

[4] Sometimes translated as thought transformation.

The text begins[5]

Homage to great compassion

The term "great compassion" may be understood on two levels: interpretive and definitive. On the interpretive level, it refers to Avalokiteshvara, the Buddha of Compassion; on the definitive level, it is the mind wanting to free all beings from suffering. This is the compassion that is important at the beginning, like a seed; in the middle, like the moisture and nutrition that make a plant grow; and at the end, like the ripening of the fruit.

The essence of this nectar of secret instruction
Is transmitted from the master from Sumatra, Serlingpa.

These two lines explain the great qualities of the teacher in order to generate confidence in the source of the mind training teachings. They originated with the Buddha himself and have come down to us today through an unbroken lineage of masters, including Serlingpa and Atisha.

Generally speaking, nectar means immortality—here it specifically indicates something that overpowers the various demonic forces that put an end to our life. Thus it actually indicates the Buddha, because the story of the Buddha tells how he overcame those forces. So when the text says "this nectar" it shows that this teaching has come from the Buddha.

---

[5] In this commentary, the root text is indented and italicized; quotations from other sources are indented but not italicized.

He actually taught the method of generating bodhicitta through equalizing and exchanging self and others in a couple of sutras where he described how he had practiced it himself in previous lives. This teaching on exchanging self and others then passed down from master to master until it reached the great Nagarjuna, who wrote in his text, the *Precious Garland of the Middle Way*,

May the negativity and suffering of others ripen on me
And may all my virtue and happiness ripen on them.[6]

Buddha Maitreya also taught it in his *Ornament for the Mahayana Sutras* and Asanga taught it in his seven treatises on the levels, specifically in his *Bodhisattva Levels*. Moreover, Shantideva taught this subject very clearly in his *Guide to the Bodhisattva Way of Life*, where he explained exactly what equalizing and exchanging self and others means. Thus this lineage shows that this teaching comes from an authentic source—the Buddha—and is not something newly fabricated.

The root text continues:

You should understand the significance of this instruction
As like a diamond, the sun and a medicinal tree.
This time of the five degenerations will then be transformed
Into the path to the fully awakened state.

---

[6] *Buddhist Advice for Living and Liberation*, page 162, verse 484.

This section, an explanation of the greatness of the text, is designed to excite our interest in it. The second line says "like a diamond, the sun and a medicinal tree," the Tibetan word *dorje* [Skt: *vajra*] being translated as "diamond" here. Even a small fragment of diamond is more valuable than gold or other precious substances, so a diamond is said to outshine them all. Similarly, even a small, partial instruction from the *Seven-Point Mind Training* is exceptionally powerful and very effective for destroying our selfishness, and in that way it surpasses all other kinds of teaching.

Then it says that mind training is like the sun. Of course, when the sun is up and fully visible in the sky it completely illuminates the land, but even before it has actually arisen its light dispels much of the darkness of the night. Similarly, even when we understand or practice only a part of mind training it is already very powerful in overcoming selfishness and the other delusions.

Finally, mind training is likened to a medicinal tree, whose roots, trunk, branches, flowers and leaves are all therapeutic, making the whole tree medicinal. Therefore, while of course the whole tree can cure disease, even one of its leaves or petals is similarly effective, and in the same way, even a partial explanation of this mind training is very powerful in overcoming the negative mind.

Therefore, just as diamonds, the sun and medicinal trees are regarded as important and precious, so, too, is this mind training teaching.

The last two lines of this verse say "This time of the five degenerations will then be transformed into the path to the fully awakened state." Without going into the time of the five degenerations in detail, it refers to a period such as the present, when people's minds and activities have degenerated.[7] For instance, even though we have used our mind to make incredible technological advances—for example, we have harnessed nuclear power with all its positive uses—we have also used that very same intelligence to create weapons of mass destruction.

Somehow, ours is a time of fear, and in that sense it is degenerate. Nuclear power stations can be very dangerous if they malfunction and nuclear weapons obviously threaten us all. There are many adverse circumstances within our external environment and our own minds and bodies that likewise cause us many problems. At such times it is very easy for practitioners to completely abandon their practice. If we fail to respond to such difficulties properly we will experience only negative consequences.

We're liable to face many dangerous and harmful situations where not only do we risk giving up even trying to practice Dharma but sometimes things are so bad that we end up killing ourselves. Usually we're very fond of ourselves—nobody cares for us as much as we do—but when the going gets rough some of us even kill ourselves.

Therefore, instead of just letting things be, we need to find a method that enables us to transform unfavorable conditions into a support for our practice and not let them stop us from doing it altogether.

[7] The five degenerations are those of life span, view, delusion, sentient beings and time. See *Advice from a Spiritual Friend*, pp. 86–7, for a brief description.

· · · 3 · · ·

The First Point: The Preliminaries
as a Basis for the Practice

S O FAR we have looked at the source of this instruction and its qualities. This section shows how the teacher should lead students
through the instruction. Because the text explains the practice in seven
sections, it is called the *Seven-Point Mind Training*.

The first of the seven points is stated in the line

First, train in the preliminaries.

While mind training is a practice of the person of great scope, it depends
upon the preliminaries, which are practices explained mainly for per-
sons of small and middle scopes. There are four. The practices for a person of small scope are thinking about

(a) the precious human life—how difficult to achieve and valuable it is;

(b) impermanence—in the sense of meditating mindfully on
death; and

(c) refuge and karma—the explanation of karma and its results is
the advice we should follow after going for refuge.

The practices for a person of middle scope, which are based on the above, are mainly

(d) meditating on the faults and sufferings of cyclic existence.

However, we don't have time here to discuss all these small and middle scope preliminary practices in detail.[8]

---

[8] For detailed teachings on all three scopes see, for example, *The Great Treatise on the Stages of the Path to Enlightenment* and *Liberation in the Palm of Your Hand.*

··· 4 ···

The Second Point: The Actual Practice, Training in Bodhicitta

FOR PRACTITIONERS of great scope, the main point is the method of meditating on or practicing bodhicitta—the determination to achieve enlightenment for the sake of all sentient beings. What does this mean? Bodhicitta is a primary mind associated with two aspirations—the first, its cause, is what we practice to generate bodhicitta, the aspiration to benefit all sentient beings; the second, which accompanies and is similar to bodhicitta, is the aspiration to achieve enlightenment.

So, bodhicitta is a primary mind accompanied by the aspiration for enlightenment for the sake of all sentient beings. There are three kinds of enlightenment—those of the hearer, solitary realizer and bodhisattva. Bodhicitta aspires to the highest form of enlightenment, that of the bodhisattva—the great, or Mahayana, enlightenment. When we understand that bodhicitta is the aspiration to attain the highest kind of enlightenment and that hearers and solitary realizers do not have it, we should feel strongly motivated to achieve enlightenment for the sake of all sentient beings because of the many unbearable sufferings they experience within cyclic existence.

We should also recognize that we are impermanent, changing from moment to moment, and must eventually leave this life, as we cannot stay here forever. Furthermore, when we do leave this life, even though we might have accumulated enough wealth and possessions to completely fill the whole Earth, we can take absolutely nothing with us and have to leave it all behind. Even if we have a huge family with hundreds of thousands of relatives, we will have to relinquish them all; not one can accompany us. Even this body, which we have inhabited since we entered our mother's womb and have taken so much care of all our life, will not help us but will be left behind. Understanding all this should encourage us to practice and try to generate bodhicitta right away.

Of course, generating bodhicitta will not protect us from death, but if we *do* generate this attitude—or even if we simply practice it—we will not die a normal death; we will die with joy. That's the difference bodhicitta makes. Normally, as we age, we find it difficult to stand up—we have to haul ourselves up on a stick or push against something solid—and when we sit down we just flop down into the chair. It's difficult to do anything. But if we have developed bodhicitta, we'll at least know that death is going to bring us a nice new body and will feel very positive about dying.

I speak from personal experience about the suffering of old age. I tell you, if you went to bed one night and woke up the next morning old, with all its attendant sufferings, you'd find it totally unbearable. However, the special sufferings of old age creep up on us gradually, and those who have had plenty of positive experiences from practicing bodhicitta are quite happy to die because it's a chance to get rid of their rubbishy old body and move into one in which it will be much easier to practice. People who die without having practiced Dharma feel very afraid.

There are two kinds of bodhicitta—conventional and ultimate. Certain earlier presentations of how to generate it explained how to develop ultimate bodhicitta first and then moved on to conventional bodhicitta, but some recent masters have said that this is incorrect and that instead we should begin with conventional bodhicitta and then practice the ultimate. This is the order of the version presented here; the tradition that put ultimate bodhicitta first was taught for practitioners of extremely sharp intellect.

The training in conventional bodhicitta is explained here principally by way of the technique of equalizing and exchanging self and others. The other method, the sevenfold cause and effect instruction, is partly relevant, but equalizing and exchanging self and others is what is mainly explained. In his *Compendium of Training*, Shantideva says that our bodhicitta will be much firmer if we develop it by practicing equalizing and exchanging self and others from the outset.

Equalizing self and others

What exactly does equalizing self and others mean? Specifically, what is it that is supposed to be equalized? For example, is it that self and others are equal in being selfless, lacking in self-existence? Although this is true, it's not what is meant here. Is it that self and others are equal in suffering in cyclic existence? Again, although this is true as well, neither is that our focus here. Perhaps the meaning is that self and others are equal in wanting happiness and not wanting suffering? The answer here is yes, self and others are indeed the same in wanting happiness and not wanting suffering, and this is what we are talking about here.

When we talk about equalizing self and others in order to generate bodhicitta, what we mean by the equality of self and others is that we all want happiness and none of us wants suffering.

Since time without beginning we have harbored the selfish attitude that continually makes us afraid of getting cold, hungry, thirsty and so forth or suffering in other ways. We always worry about what will happen to us. This continual worry is the selfishness that's called the self-cherishing mind—the tendency to focus on our own happiness while neglecting the welfare and needs of others—and we have been under its influence since beginningless time.

Exchanging self and others means switching these two so that instead of being primarily concerned about our own happiness we become more concerned for that of others, and instead of neglecting others we neglect ourselves and strive for enlightenment for their benefit.

There is a connection between the self-cherishing mind and self-grasping, or grasping at true existence. The self-grasping mind is the actual root, or fundamental cause, of all samsaric suffering but it is very closely followed by the self-cherishing mind, which arises on the basis of self-grasping and itself serves as the basis for all the other delusions.

There are said to be 84,000 delusions, each of which arises as a result of the self-cherishing mind. Motivated by these delusions, we engage in harmful actions such as the ten non-virtuous actions,[9] the five immediate negativities[10] and other kinds of negative activity and,

---

[9] Three of body (killing, stealing and sexual misconduct), four of speech (lying, slandering, speaking harshly and gossiping) and three of mind (covetousness, ill-will and wrong views).
[10] Killing father, mother or an arhat, drawing blood from a buddha and creating a schism in the Sangha community. They are called immediate because those who create such actions are reborn in hell in their very next life.

as a karmic consequence of doing so, have to undergo all kinds of unbearable suffering.

Thus the very root, the fundamental cause, of all our delusions, negative minds and suffering is self-grasping, the mind that thinks we are completely self-existent, inherently-existent; that we exist in a way that is totally independent of any causes or conditions, utterly independent of anything.

And if self-grasping is the king, then self-cherishing is his most powerful minister, the one who tries to achieve all kinds of objectives on his behalf. Selfishness itself does not conceive of or believe in the self as existing from its own side because that is not its job. However, the selfish mind does act as a protector or helper for the self that is conceived of by self-grasping as existing from its own side.

In order to get nice things for the self, self-cherishing causes us to develop attachment; to protect the self from harm, self-cherishing causes us to generate anger; in other situations it stimulates jealousy, pride and other delusions. Then, by following these negative minds, we engage in negative actions, create negative karma and suffer. Thus selfishness is just like a minister that the king can order around to get whatever he wants done.

Therefore, we should think repeatedly about how self-cherishing creates all our suffering and problems until we see it as our main enemy. Then, instead of allowing selfishness, whose main aim is our own happiness, to lead us around by the nose, we should switch everything around and start thinking about how we can benefit others, how their happiness is more important than our own.

If we think about it correctly we can easily understand how important others are and how all our happiness and fortune definitely and completely depend on them.

I mentioned before that one way of developing bodhicitta is through the sevenfold cause and effect instruction, which, based on equanimity, is as follows:

(a) recognizing that all beings have been our mother,

(b) recollecting their kindness as mother,

(c) thinking how to repay their kindness,

(d) developing love,

(e) developing compassion,

(f) generating the special intention of benefiting all beings by oneself alone, and then

(g) generating bodhicitta itself.

The only way we can gain these realizations is by depending on others.

Likewise, the only way we can develop the six perfections of generosity, morality, patience, enthusiasm, concentration and wisdom is by depending on others. Take, for example, the practice of generosity, the mind wanting to give away all our possessions and even our body in order to benefit others. Obviously we can do this only in dependence upon others; it is only thanks to them that we can develop a generous mind.

Then there's morality, which means abandoning the ten non-virtuous actions—killing, stealing, lying and so forth. Abandoning killing means giving up taking the lives of others; we can do this only by depending upon others; again, it is only thanks to them that we can do it. Similarly, we abandon stealing by regarding others as important and therefore not taking their possessions; it is only thanks to others that we can do this, too. The same applies to all other beneficial qualities of mind—we can develop them only through the kindness of others.

We should think, therefore, that we must definitely attain the state of complete enlightenment as soon as possible for the sake of all sentient beings, and for that reason determine to spend all our time from now on working towards that goal without wasting even a moment. We must resolve to practice like this in particular for whatever remains of this life—studying, thinking, meditating and practicing as well as we can—especially this year, this month, this week and particularly this day. We must generate the strong determination to not waste time but spend every moment practicing whatever we have to do to attain enlightenment as quickly as possible.

Meditation on equalizing self and others is done by way of nine reasons, of which six work on the conventional level and three on the ultimate. With respect to the six conventional ones, three relate to self and three to others. This is how we should meditate on the equality of self and others.[11]

---

[11] *Transforming Adversity Into Joy And Courage*, pp. 167–71. This entire book, especially chapters 10–12, augments Geshe Tegchok's thoughts on the development and practice of bodhicitta.

The shortcomings of self-cherishing

The fourth paragraph of the text says,

Banish the one to blame for everything,
Meditate on the great kindness of all beings.

The first line means that we should blame the self-cherishing mind for all our negative experiences. Why? Because every problem and fault we experience is a result of our own selfishness. Therefore we should blame ourselves for every unpleasant experience that befalls us, no matter how bad it is; we should grab hold of our own selfish mind and view it as the culprit.

As the great Shantideva wrote in his *Guide,*

All the suffering in the world
Comes from the desire for one's own happiness.[12]

Every problem we experience comes from wanting and thinking of only our own happiness; all our suffering—everything that goes wrong, every kind of fault, everything fearful or unpleasant and all violence—comes from this selfish mind. Furthermore, it all comes equally from the self-grasping mind that conceives everything to exist from its own side.

Shantideva then compares selfishness to an extremely harmful spirit that continuously harms us.

[12] *A Guide to the Bodhisattva Way of Life,* Chapter 8, verse 129 (p. 106, note 297).

If all the harm, fear and suffering in the world

Occur due to grasping onto the self,

What use is that great demon to me?[13]

Thus we're encouraged to ask ourselves, "Why do I hang on to this self-ish mind, which is such a harmful entity?"

As the Indian master Padampa Sangye told the people of Tingri, where he had decided to stay because he felt he could help them, whenever things go wrong we always blame others but we should instead point the finger of blame at ourselves, where the root of all problems lies.[14]

And, as the mind training text The Wheel-Weapon Mind Training says, if we develop this understanding it is marvelous, because by so doing we identify the real enemy that continuously gives us harm—beginning, middle and end. It says, "So now I've identified you, you thief."[15]

But self-cherishing is not the ordinary kind of thief, who robs people by beating them up and forcibly taking their possessions. Self-cherishing is the type of thief that sneaks in surreptitiously at night and steals on the sly.

The Wheel-Weapon also says, "So now I've understood you for what you are, you unfaithful friend!"[16] From the point of view of our own

[13] Ibid. Chapter 8, verse 134 (p. 106, note 300).
[14] "You say such clever things to people, but don't apply them to yourself; People of Tingri, the faults within you are the ones to be exposed." Dilgo Khyentse. The Hundred Verses of Advice of Padampa Sangye. Boston: Shambhala Publications, 2002, verse 89.
[15] Peacock in the Poison Grove, p. 83, verse 49: "I seize the thief who ambushed and deceived me."
[16] Ibid. Same verse: "The hypocrite who deceived me disguised as myself."

selfishness it seems to be our greatest friend, but in practice it does nothing but trick and deceive us. The selfish mind creates all the suffering we
experience in this life, such as people being horrible to us, hitting and
attacking us with weapons, but more especially, it is the cause of all the
unbearable sufferings we're going to experience in the lower realms in
our future lives.

As Shantideva also said, look at the difference between the buddhas
and ordinary worldly people like ourselves.[17] Because we have not yet dis-
carded our selfishness, we are still suffering here in cyclic existence, not
even free from rebirth in the lower realms. Even arhats, who have completely transcended the suffering of cyclic existence, have reached only
a limited degree of perfection because they have not relinquished their
selfishness. They have not devoted themselves to benefiting others; therefore they have not been able to achieve the state of full enlightenment.

The Buddha, on the other hand, gave up all selfishness and totally
devoted himself to benefiting others. As a result, he reached a state of
complete freedom from suffering and to this day remains incredibly
beneficial to and highly regarded by many beings. By seeing the difference between him and us, we will understand how important it is also
to renounce the selfish mind and totally devote ourselves to benefiting
others.

Originally, the Buddha was exactly the same as us. When water is
boiling, the water on the top goes to the bottom and the water on the
bottom comes up to the top, and it keeps on going round like that. Similarly, in many previous lives we were together with the Buddha—some-

---

[17] Op. cit. Chapter 8, verse 130: "Enough of much talk! Note the difference between the
fool who seeks his own benefit and the sage who works for the benefit of others."

times as best friends, sometimes as worst enemies, all the time changing, changing, changing. Then, unlike us, at a certain point he decided to enter the path by renouncing selfishness and devoting himself to others, and kept on developing spiritually until he attained enlightenment.

The kindness of all sentient beings

Furthermore, Shantideva pointed out that everything good—every form of happiness, all positive qualities and so forth—comes through the kindness of others. Therefore, the mind devoted to their welfare is like a wish-fulfilling jewel, the source of all happiness and everything good and useful in the world. Just as a farmer who possesses an extremely fertile field, where everything he plants always grows, is very happy to have it and cherishes and takes great care of it, we should feel the same way about other sentient beings—that they are extremely valuable, and cherish and take care of them.

It is interesting that, whether we are Buddhist or not, if we think about the great kindness of all beings it will be evident that all our happiness does indeed depend upon them.

It is also said that the buddhas and sentient beings are equally kind. The buddhas' kindness is obvious—through following their teachings and advice we can attain enlightenment. However, we do so only by meditating on love, compassion, bodhicitta, the six perfections, the four means of taking care of disciples and so forth, and doing these practices obviously depends upon others. Therefore, they and the buddhas are equally kind and it is wrong to dismiss sentient beings while holding the buddhas in great esteem.

This does not mean that we should make prostrations, offerings, prayers and requests to sentient beings to be able to generate realizations and so forth but that they and the buddhas are equally important and kind in the genesis of our happiness and we should therefore appreciate and respect them both equally.

Having understood that all happiness, especially the many qualities we are trying to develop on the Mahayana path to enlightenment, results from the kindness of not just the buddhas but also all sentient beings, from this point on we should always remember how all beings are kind. This is what "meditate on the great kindness of all beings" means.

When we think about self and others, self refers to just the one person whereas others are utterly uncountable. Nevertheless, we normally take tremendous care of that one self and basically ignore most of the others. If we think about the difference in numbers here, it seems disgraceful to ignore the numberless in favor of just the one whereas neglecting the one in favor of the countless others doesn't seem so bad.

As soon as we start meditating on all beings as most kind, even though we can concentrate on love and compassion—wanting all beings to be happy and free from suffering—for only a very short time, it is still a very powerful way of building up an extraordinary amount of merit. That's why meditation on qualities such as love and compassion is so valuable.

Of course, it is inevitable and to be expected that we beginners meditating on the kindness of all sentient beings will occasionally create negative karma by getting angry at some of them, therefore we also need to know how to purify immediately any negativity we create.

According to the sevenfold cause and effect instruction, above, when we meditate on the four immeasurables, which include love—wishing all beings to be happy—and compassion—wishing them to be free from suffering—and on bodhicitta—the determination to achieve enlightenment for the sake of all sentient beings—we start by recognizing all beings as having been our mother, recollecting their kindness and resolving to repay this kindness, and then go on to meditate on love, compassion, the special intention and finally the mind of bodhicitta itself. All these recognitions and qualities arise through the kindness of others because it is only by meditating on others that we can generate them.

Once we have entered the path to enlightenment we develop it further by practicing the six perfections and so forth. Again, each of these depends on the kindness of others. When we finally achieve enlightenment we spend all our time benefiting others because of the strength of our compassion, which cannot bear to see or ignore others' suffering. So again, even when we become buddha, all our enlightened activity depends upon others and their kindness.

A mother's kindness

Simply by looking at our present life we can see the kindness of others. From conception we were completely reliant on our mother's kindness for survival. For the nine months we were in her womb she underwent many difficulties carrying us and then faced the hardships of giving us birth. Then, when we were very small, there was no way we could look after ourselves—we were always in danger of falling or getting hurt in various other ways, and when we got a bit bigger we were again in danger of running into traffic, falling from high places and so forth.

Parents constantly have to think about their children, protect them from danger and work to feed and educate them and so forth. Thus when we were small we completely depended on the kindness of our parents for everything.

This is also true for animals. We can see how ducks and geese, for example, look after their young—and while there is actually very little they can do to protect them from predators they will nevertheless defend them with their lives.

As we get older and go to school, our education depends upon the kindness of our teachers and our fun depends upon the kindness of the other children we play with. Later on, when we get married, start a family, live together and so forth, our enjoyment of all this going smoothly and happily depends upon our partner and the other members of our family. And when we become old and find it difficult to sit or stand and can't cook or take care of ourselves properly, we again need somebody to look after us.

Thus, it's clear that from the beginning of our life to its end, even our mundane happiness depends entirely upon the kindness of others, and not only the kindness of other human beings—we use animals' bodies for food, shoes and clothing and so forth and they keep us company, protect us and help us in our work. Therefore we should also appreciate the kindness of animals.

With respect to other kinds of food, consider how grain used for food starts off in dependence on the kindness of others. Somebody plants the seeds in a field; somebody tills the earth; somebody removes the weeds; many people harvest the crop and make it ready to cook; others mill the flour and make bread; somebody else prepares our rice. Thus everything we eat depends on the kindness of the many others who bring it to us. Furthermore, the roads that bring us our food and help us get from place to place were built by the hard work of many people.

We might think that we paid for all this, but where did we get the money? It came from our job, but we only got that because somebody gave it to us.

Therefore, all we have comes from the kindness of others. We came into this world completely naked, without a stitch of clothing or anything in our hands. All we have accumulated since then has come from others.

We must reflect from our own experience on all the other ways in which others have been kind to us. The more we think about this, the more embarrassed we'll be at thinking of ourselves as important and precious, and the more we'll realize that in fact it is others who are important and precious. If we don't think deeply about all this, it won't make much sense, but if we want to follow the spiritual path we must develop this awareness. Meditating on the kindness of others is priceless.

Giving and taking

The next line of the text says,

Practice a combination of giving and taking.

This means that we should alternate giving and taking [Tib: *tong-len*]. I've been talking about the kindness of others—the more we think about this the more we'll realize the extent of their suffering and will come to think that it's so terrible that we must do something about it. Eventually we'll feel compelled to take their suffering on ourselves and give them our happiness. This is what giving and taking means—giving happiness to all beings and taking on all their suffering—and we practice it in an attempt to destroy our self-cherishing mind.

We might think that since the suffering of others does not hurt us, why even consider taking it on? In response, the commentary reminds us that even in their *dreams* all beings want happiness and do not want suffering.

We might also think that while it is true that we all want happiness and freedom from suffering, nevertheless, the best thing is simply to take care of our own happiness and eliminate our own suffering. Moreover, we might wonder whether it is even *possible* to give happiness to others and alleviate their suffering, arguing that, since each of us has our own individual mind stream, we can of course create happiness in and remove suffering from our own mind, but how can we possibly do this for others? After all, their minds are completely separate from ours; surely they must be responsible for creating their own happiness and eliminating their own suffering?

While it is true that our minds are separate, it still makes sense that one person can help another find happiness and freedom from suffering. For example, a mother and her child are responsible for helping each other find happiness and eliminate problems.

Now, we might argue that even though mother and child have different mindstreams, because they are so close and have great affection for one another it's possible to talk of *their* doing this but not other sentient beings. The answer is that although it is true that in this life we have only one mother and father and don't have that special connection with other sentient beings, before this life there was a previous one, and before that there was another, and before that another and so on—in fact, there is no beginning to the lives we have had in cyclic existence.

Furthermore, in many of those lives we were born from a womb, just as we were in this one, and if we think deeply about this we will see that every single living being has been our mother and father and has therefore been extremely kind to us. Through reflecting on the kindness of our present mother and father we should understand that in past lives, when other beings were our parents, they were similarly kind and affectionate towards us. Perhaps they were even kinder, sometimes even giving up their very life for our sake.

Thus all sentient beings have helped us in countless ways and saved us from innumerable harms and have even given their life for us on numberless occasions. However, the selfish mind says that while all this might be true, it happened so long ago that it's all forgotten by now. Moreover, it also says that many of these beings have actually done their best to harm us as much as they can, so caring for all beings is out of the question.

However, the commentary points out that it is only our own selfishness that is raising these objections and denying the need to think so much about others and describes this way of thinking as a debate between selfishness and the altruistic mind dedicated to benefiting others. It's like a dramatization, which is actually how to reflect and meditate. It discusses potential objections our mind might raise when we think about these issues, several of which will ring true to our experience. When the selfish mind comes up with these objections we have to find a way to respond.

For instance, when the selfish mind asserts that many other people are intent on harming us, the altruistic mind retorts that this is unreasonable because since beginningless time, over countless lifetimes in cyclic existence, others have been extremely kind to us. We cannot possibly measure how kind they have all been or count how many times they have protected and helped us. They have shown us this kindness since beginningless time and now, because of some minor problem, we're branding certain people worst enemies undeserving of help. This is completely unreasonable and we should be ashamed of ourselves for even thinking it. Don't we feel even a little embarrassed by our reaction?

Our ways of thinking and behaving are profoundly ignorant and particularly unpleasant because they completely disregard the untold help we have received and merely remember the little harm. It's as if our parents, having taken care of us all our life, have become old and sick and gone into hospital and then said just one unpleasant thing to us, and we have reacted with anger and attacked them. If our family and friends would come to know how we have completely forgotten our parents' kindness and reacted with hatred just because of this one comment they would be disgusted at our behavior.

Moreover, we may wonder why we meditate on the kindness of others and take on their suffering because neither we nor they seem to be affected by this practice. To this we can reply that of course no immediately visible, direct effects arise from such practice, any more than they do when we make offerings, prostrations and so forth to the buddhas, which also bring no immediate result. It is different when we give food or drink to those who are hungry or thirsty because such actions bring immediate benefit. But when we do this, do we really experience no benefit? Do we ourselves derive no benefit at all? We might feel that we do not benefit personally from giving to others in this way, at least not directly or immediately, but that doesn't mean there's no result at all. Likewise, if we see no immediate, visible result from practicing morality, does that mean that moral conduct has no benefit at all?

With respect to the karma created by various actions, some actions bring results in this life, some in the next and certain others in a more distant future life. Therefore, the altruistic mind has to respond to the selfish mind's objection above by saying, "You are rather stupid in failing to recognize that the good you do might *not* bring immediate results. For example, farmers plant various kinds of seed, some of which ripen that very year, others the following year and some only several years later. The fact that they don't all bring immediate results doesn't stop the farmer from planting them."

Likewise, when we try to generate, meditate on and practice bodhicitta, we don't necessarily experience immediate, visible results like those of eating when we're hungry, but nevertheless, the future good results that will eventually ripen are endless.

Just as when we see a high quality crop we can infer that its seeds must have been excellent, in the same way, when we see any good result we can confidently infer that it must have had a good cause. The principle that good results must be preceded by good causes applies to the state of enlightenment itself.

The exalted state of enlightenment—in which all good qualities are fully developed and from which all faults and obscurations are totally absent—is a good result. We can therefore infer that it must have been preceded by many good causes, such as the practice of the six perfections and the four means of taking care of disciples and so forth, and we can speak of all such practices along the path, over an extremely long period of time, as the good causes that bring the great result of enlightenment.

Thus we can see that by using our wisdom and intelligence to understand the difference between right and wrong and gradually working at eliminating wrong, harmful states of mind and actions and developing correct, beneficial ones, over time, we can attain enlightenment. Once we have done so we will be able to benefit many, many beings extensively—ripen on the path those not yet ripened, liberate those not liberated and completely free from all obscurations those not yet free. How will we be able to do that? How do enlightened beings do that? While on the path they gradually develop the mind wanting to benefit others, practice actions beneficial to others and abandon all thoughts and actions harmful to others, thereby gradually acquiring the power to attain the omniscient mind of a buddha.

That is the ultimate result, but the benefits of the actions that bring it are not seen immediately, unlike those of eating and drinking to get rid of hunger and thirst. In response to this, the selfish mind might reply, "That's OK, ultimately there might be such a result, but for the time being I'm not interested in trying to benefit all sentient beings because it's evident that however much I look at it, I see little benefit to either my body or my mind."

However, this thought is also a mistake because, even in the short term, there are many benefits from helping others and not harming them. When we live trying to be as helpful to others as we can and avoiding aggressive, negative mental attitudes and actions towards them, our companions and the people with whom we live really appreciate us because our behavior makes them happy and we in turn enjoy being appreciated, popular and well-liked.

Although the selfish mind does not understand and appreciate all this, the buddhas, bodhisattvas and other holy beings do. Similarly, those of us who are trying to develop, practice and meditate on love, compassion and so forth also understand and appreciate it, as do the people with whom we spend our lives, as I've just said. Even strangers with whom we've just come into contact will appreciate and take a liking to us. They feel something right away, just as we immediately feel uncomfortable and afraid the moment we encounter a vicious, violent person, even somebody we've never seen before, or a scorpion or poisonous snake.

The selfish mind might further object that there's no point in meditating on love or compassion because there's no direct personal physical or mental benefit. The reply to this is, "Normally you, the selfish mind, say all sorts of unpleasant things to people—perhaps you should give up doing this because it harms neither their bodies nor their minds; so why bother? Moreover, you are normally so full of malevolent thoughts and covetousness towards others—perhaps you should give these thoughts up as well; since they neither help nor harm anybody directly, physically or mentally, just forget them." It's only when you take *action* on the basis of your ill will or covetousness that you actually harm others physically, so since those attitudes themselves neither harm nor help others directly, why not just drop them?

Such objections can arise when we think deeply about the various disadvantages of the selfish mind and begin to gain experience in this area. One lama explored this issue in his writings and, although it wasn't in relation to the text we're studying here, I'll use what he said to illustrate the following point. Debating with the selfish mind about these things until it has nothing left to say is extremely helpful.

To continue the argument, then, the selfish mind objects: "I don't want to practice altruism or give up selfishness because doing so has no direct benefit." The reply to this is that we readily accept the benefits of saving money and other things for our old age but since doing so has no direct or immediate benefit us, why bother? Similarly, if we get a thorn in our foot, our hand removes it; since this does not benefit our hand in any way, why should it bother to help the foot?

If we do not abandon selfishness and devote ourselves to the happiness and welfare of others we will never achieve the perfect happiness of enlightenment and will forever be stuck with changeable, unreliable kinds of happiness.

How to practice giving and taking

The text then goes on to say,

Giving and taking should be practiced alternately.

First we were told to practice a combination of giving and taking; now we're being told to practice them alternately. Finally,

And you should begin by taking from yourself.

Thus these two lines tell us how to practice giving and taking, the second being for those of us who lack the courage to practice taking in its fullest form—taking on all suffering of all beings—straight away. We build up to it gradually by taking on our own suffering first. How do we do this?

We can start by meditating each morning on taking on, in advance, the suffering we're going to experience that day. On that basis we gradually build up to taking on the suffering of the next day as well, then the day after that, and so on until we're able to take on all the suffering of this life and finally, the suffering of all our future lives.

Once we can do this we extend the taking to all our friends and relatives, then gradually build up to include all the people to whom we feel neutral, those who are neither friends nor enemies, and when we've mastered that we add in our enemies, those who harm us, thus extending our practice to include all sentient beings. Of course, if we have the courage and strength of mind to practice this most difficult technique from the outset we don't need to train our mind in the gradual method that begins with taking on our own suffering first.

Briefly, in a simplified way, the meditation on taking is as follows.

Reflect on the six realms of cyclic existence: the hell, hungry ghost, animal, human, demigod and god realms.[18]

Within the hell realm lie the hot and cold hells. The hot hells have eight levels with progressively increasing suffering, as do the cold hells. After the first level, the second has more suffering, the third still more, and so on. Then there are the surrounding hells like the hell of the *shalmali* tree,

---

[18] See the relevant sections of *Liberation in the Palm of Your Hand* for details of all these.

the swamps of rotting corpses and so forth, and then the temporary hells as well. However, the main sufferings that we take from the hell beings are those of the intense heat and cold they endure.

The worst sufferings in all of cyclic existence are those of the hell beings. The hungry ghosts experience slightly less and the animals' sufferings are somewhat less again. The principal sufferings that the hungry ghosts undergo are those of hunger and thirst; they can go millions of years without finding even a gob of spit to eat.

With respect to the animals, if we look at those who live among us, especially in the West compared to Asia, they seem quite well cared for. Sometimes it can look as if pet dogs and cats, and even livestock, have an enjoyable life. They get a pleasant place to sleep and their food is prepared for them; it's often better than that of humans in many parts of the world. The animals that live among us—pets, livestock and so forth—are referred to as "scattered animals" and compared to other animals actually suffer less than the majority, who live in the oceans.

Nowadays films give us a glimpse of how sea creatures live in water teeming with different species of fish; thousands, even millions, of different creatures living there together. They have more suffering than most land animals.

The general suffering of animals is that of not being aware and of eating and being eaten by each other. The big ones prey on the smaller ones or sometimes the smaller ones gang up on the big ones and kill and eat them instead. This goes on all the time and causes great suffering.

When taking suffering from humans, think about the three, six or eight sufferings. For example, the eight include the sufferings of birth, aging, sickness, and death; of not being able to get what we want; of being separated from things and people we love; of all sorts of unwanted unpleasant things happening to us; and of our physical and mental aggregates, which are under the control of delusion and karma.

The main suffering of the demigods is that of fighting. Out of jealousy, they constantly fight with the gods, who eat the fruit of a tree whose roots are in the realm of the demigods but ripens in the realm of the gods.

The gods live for millions and millions of years, enjoying themselves greatly, experiencing extraordinary pleasure with their divine friends, but at the end of their lives, a week before they die, they hear a sound like an announcement in space, telling them that they will die on such and such a day. From that point on their splendor fades, they start to smell and their friends no longer want to come anywhere near them. Furthermore, they become aware that they have exhausted their merit and will soon be reborn in the lower realms.

Therefore, in that final week of their lives, they experience dreadful suffering, which is made more intense by seeing that all their pleasure is coming to an end and that they are about to experience great suffering. Moreover, even though a week might not sound like much, a week in the life of a god is like billions of years in the human realm.

The three lower realms are called bad realms because their inhabitants create nothing but bad actions and experience only bad results, while the three upper realms are called good realms because their inhabitants experience good results of good actions.[19]

---

[19] The three upper realms are still fraught with all kinds of samsaric suffering (like the three, six and eight) but are relatively happier than the lower realms, therefore they are called "good."

When we practice tong-len[20] we begin by imagining the hell realms, thinking about the terrible sufferings the hell beings experience, and visualize taking it all on, completely relieving them of it all. Once we have done this we imagine giving the hell beings all our possessions, happiness and merit, the receipt of which brings each hell being to complete enlightenment. We then gradually work our way up in a similar manner through the other realms.

The way to practice taking is to concentrate on our breath and imagine that the sufferings of the beings in the particular realm we're focusing on leave through their right nostril and enter us through our right. Visualizing our selfish-cherishing mind as a dense blackness at our heart chakra in the center of our chest, the sufferings we inhale descend dissolve into it, completely destroying this selfish mind.

The way to practice giving is to imagine sending out through our left nostril our entire body and all our possessions, happiness and merit from the past, present and future to each and every sentient being in the realm we're focusing on. All this enters their left nostril, as a result of which they develop all the realizations on the path and become fully enlightened.

After taking on all the sufferings of the hell beings and using them to harm our selfish mind and then giving them all our happiness and so forth, bringing them to complete enlightenment, we move on to the hungry ghosts. We likewise take all their suffering from their right nostril into our right nostril; it too dissolves into and destroys our self-cherishing mind. We then send out all our happiness, merit and so forth

[20] For a highly detailed description of this practice see Meditation Seven in Lama Zopa Rinpoche's *Wish-Fulfilling Golden Sun* on the LYWA Web site: www.LamaYeshe.com.

through our left nostril; it enters their left nostril and brings them to enlightenment.

When giving, we should feel as if we're turning on a light in a dark place. It might have been dark for thousands or even millions of years, but no matter how long the darkness has been there, as soon as we turn on the light it's immediately dispelled. In the same way, when we send our happiness and merit from our left nostril into the beings in the realm we're focusing on, even though all their obscurations and so forth might have been there for a long time, they are totally eliminated and those beings are established in the state of complete enlightenment.

Thus, we gradually go through this process with all six types of sentient beings up to the gods, taking on their suffering, using it to destroy our selfish mind.

We can sometimes add another visualization to this practice: after bringing all beings to enlightenment we receive back through our left nostril the blessings of their enlightened body, speech and mind. These blessings completely eliminate our self-grasping mind—which resides in our heart and has always believed that everything exists from its own side, independent of all causes and conditions—like switching on a light instantly dispels darkness from a room or a powerful jet of water immediately sweeps away a pile of dirt.

Meditating like this is a way of taking action. Instead of merely generating the aspirational love that wishes all beings to be happy and the compassion that wishes them all to be free from suffering, by practicing tong-len we're actively doing something that creates an extremely powerful, positive force within us.

Again, the selfish mind will raise arguments against this practice: "It's just too tiring and difficult," "What's the point? It benefits neither others nor myself" and so forth. The objection that it does not benefit us is easily refuted: it clearly strengthens our love and compassion and when we engage in this practice we can see that it creates a tremendous positive force in our mind.

With respect to the objection that this practice does not help others in any way either, once more the selfish mind is considering that the only way to help others is directly; for example, by giving them food or drink when they are hungry or thirsty. It's true that tong-len does not benefit others in that way but there are many ways in which we do benefit beings through this meditation, albeit neither directly nor immediately.

Anyway, although helpful, the benefits of giving food to the hungry or drink to the thirsty are very limited. Tong-len, by contrast, is incredibly beneficial because it is only through practicing it and similar meditations that we can become enlightened, and when we do we'll be able to benefit numberless beings in a single moment. So, looking further ahead, the practice of this meditation offers enormous benefits to both ourselves and others.

With respect to alternating taking and giving, if meditating on taking makes you feel uncomfortable and you can't handle the idea of taking on the evil actions, bad karma and negativities of others, you can leave that part out and just do the giving. Imagine all your merit, good qualities and so forth leaving you in the form of white light, going to all sentient beings, entering them and purifying them of all their delusions and negative karma. Imagine that all this is completely purified, washed out and cleansed, leaving their body in the form of frogs, scorpions, all kinds of other insects and dirty liquid and completely disappearing into the ground.

Actually, when taking, there's no reason to feel that you're being polluted because all the negativity, bad karma and obscurations you take is poured onto your selfish mind, thereby reducing its power. So you shouldn't feel that it's polluting you. It's like peacocks eating poison— it doesn't harm them but actually enhances the brilliance of the colors in their feathers.

The text continues,

These two should be made to ride on the breath.

The two referred to here are taking and giving. Although the text says "giving [*tong*] and taking [*len*]," the actual order in which we practice is taking and giving. We first take on their suffering and then give them happiness because while sentient beings are suffering, happiness is of little immediate use to them. Therefore we take away their suffering first and then give them happiness.

When we have had some experience in this meditation we combine it with our breath. Since we are always breathing, when we breathe in we imagine we're inhaling all others' suffering and when we exhale we imagine that we're sending them all our happiness and so forth on our breath, as described above.

When Khädrub-je, one of Lama Tsong Khapa's main disciples, praised him for being so helpful to others that even his breath helped them, he was referring to this practice, where high level practitioners can combine even their normal breathing with taking and giving.

Concerning the three objects, three poisons and three virtues,

The three objects are pleasant, unpleasant and neutral objects, the three poisons are attachment, aversion and ignorance and the three virtues are the opposites of the three poisons.

For example, when we come into contact with pleasant objects we experience pleasure and as a result generate attachment to those objects. When we come into contact with unpleasant objects we generate hatred, anger or aversion. And when we come into contact with neutral objects we generate a kind of neutral mental stupidity in relation to them.

It's the same in our relationships with people. We feel attached to our friends, hatred for our enemies and, towards neutral people, "strangers," our normal ignorance simply continues unabated. If whenever we notice these delusions arising in our mind we can think to ourselves, "May all the attachment, hatred and ignorance that sentient beings experience ripen on me," we generate the three virtues.

The instruction to be followed, in short,
Is to be mindful of the practice in general,
By taking these words to heart in all activities.

In brief, the way to practice is to constantly remind ourselves of these instructions in all activities, which we can do by always remembering and reciting the words of Nagarjuna mentioned before,[21]

---

[21] See note 6 above.

May the negativity and suffering of others ripen on me
And may all my virtue and happiness ripen on them.

Just as an old person needs to lean on a stick to move around, similarly, reciting words such as these helps remind us of the main points of the Mahayana mind training and keeps us going. By leaning on these words we can remember to practice taking and giving in all our daily activities.

So far this has been a commentary on the section of the text that explains how to meditate on conventional bodhicitta—how to generate the determination to achieve enlightenment for the sake of all sentient beings. There are two methods for developing bodhicitta: the sevenfold cause and effect instruction and equalizing and exchanging self and others. This has been a brief explanation of the latter, making some basic points about equalizing and exchanging self and others.

Ultimate Bodhicitta

Now let's look at the next section of the root text.

When stability has been attained, impart the secret teaching:

Stability refers to the method side.[22] When we have gained stability in the practices of conventional bodhicitta our teacher can give us the highly secret teaching on ultimate bodhicitta.

---

[22] There are two streams of practice in the Mahayana: method—the development of bodhicitta—and wisdom—the development of the wisdom directly realizing emptiness. Like a bird needs two wings to fly, we need both method and wisdom to reach enlightenment.

Ultimate bodhicitta refers to the direct realization of emptiness, so explaining it means explaining emptiness, which here means that everything is empty of true, or inherent, existence. Nothing is truly existent; everything is empty of true existence. That is the emptiness that we must realize.

Generally speaking, all phenomena that exist can be classified as either mind, which knows objects, or objects, which are known by the mind.

The next line of the text says,

Consider all phenomena as like dreams

When external objects appear to our mind, even though they appear to be truly existent, self-existent, existing from their own side, this is not at all the case. Therefore they are likened to dreams, which also seem to be real at the time but are seen to be unreal on awakening.

Both outer and inner objects are actually empty, but still, everything appears to be truly existent. However, if something *were* truly existent, if it truly existed the way in which it appears, it would have to be completely independent of anything.

For example, external objects like mountains, trees and forests are simply combinations of different particles or atoms; periods of time, such as years, months, weeks and so forth, are likewise combinations of moments. Therefore, none of these things—external objects, time or anything else—is independent of its constituent particles, periods of time and other factors. To be truly existent they would have to be completely independent of everything else.

When we talk about something being truly existent that means it's independent of everything else. But since there's nothing like that, there's nothing that's truly existent. The reason that there's nothing completely independent, or truly existent, is because everything exists in dependence upon other factors.

Take a glass of water, for example. When we think about it, of course we know that it is dependent upon this and that, such as the various causes and conditions that have gone into producing it. If, however, instead of thinking about it we examine how it looks when it first appears to us, we'll see that it has this vivid appearance, an appearance as if it *were* totally independent of any causes, conditions or, indeed, anything at all. That is how the glass of water appears—truly existent; completely independent of everything else; totally self-existent (which are just different ways of saying the same thing).

If the glass of water were truly existent the way it appears to be, it would have to be completely independent, but when we think about it we know that it depends on many different factors and is therefore *not* truly existent, independent or self-existent—and neither is anything else we can think of. Since this applies to everything that exists, all existent phenomena are empty of true existence.

Examine the nature of unborn awareness.

This next line refers to the fact that not only its objects but also the mind itself is empty of true existence. Mind, here, refers to the six kinds of primary consciousness—visual, auditory, olfactory, gustatory, tactile and mental; all completely lack any true existence.

Where it says "unborn awareness," awareness refers to consciousness. Consciousness itself is produced in dependence upon causes and conditions and is therefore not truly existent. That means a truly existent consciousness is not produced, so a truly existent consciousness is unborn.

You can understand this by examining its very nature of being completely empty of independent existence. This shows that it is neither truly existent nor produced by or dependent upon truly existent causes and conditions. Thus we have only to examine the nature of the six consciousnesses to understand that they're unborn.

The remedy itself is released in its own place

This line refers to the fact that the wisdom understanding everything to be empty of true, independent or self-existence is the remedy to all of cyclic existence and everything that produces it.

Place the essence of the path on the nature of the basis of all

This means that because everything is empty of true existence, things are produced only from particular causes and conditions and come into existence depending upon specific factors. If things were *not* empty—in other words, if everything *were* truly existent—phenomena could not possibly come into being in dependence upon certain specific causes and conditions.

Moreover, because we can see and explain how each event is produced dependent upon its own specific causes and conditions, we can see that it is also impossible to assert that any event is truly existent.

Therefore, "essence of the path" refers to an understanding of the relationship between emptiness and dependent arising, the knowledge that because everything is empty, the various manifestations of dependent arising—things arising dependent upon various causes and conditions—are possible, and because such arisings occur, everything must be empty.

In the period between sessions, be a creator of illusions.

A creator of illusions is a conjuror who can make illusory objects appear due to a special arrangement of sticks and stones together with mantras and various other substances. When he makes things appear to his audience he also sees them but since he knows that he himself has simply conjured them up he knows that they're illusory. In the same way, even when we have directly realized emptiness, when we come out of meditation, despite our knowing that nothing exists truly, everything will still *appear* to be truly existent. We'll see things as truly existent but will know that in reality, they're not; due to the force of our experience in meditation we'll have the certainty in the post-meditation period that nothing exists truly, the way it appears.

I mentioned earlier that the self-cherishing mind completely depends upon the self-grasping mind—the consciousness that conceives or apprehends that everything is truly existent and therefore completely independent.

For example, we can figure out that a cake it is not truly existent because we know it cannot be made without ingredients—fruit, butter, flour and so forth—but still, the self-grasping mind sees the cake, like everything else, to be completely truly existent and independent of any causes and conditions. This is in total conflict with the knowledge that everything exists depending upon causes and conditions and in this way, the self-grasping mind completely prevents the arising of any awareness of cause and effect, such as happiness resulting from virtue and suffering from non-virtue.

All the problems we experience in life and, indeed, all our beginning-less suffering in cyclic existence, can be traced back to our self-cherishing mind and if we delve even deeper we'll find that beneath this lies the very root of all our problems, the self-grasping mind.

Those with less experience of Buddhist teachings should try hard to understand this important point—the self-grasping mind that conceives everything as being completely independent is the support for the self-cherishing mind, which produces the various delusions that cause us to create negative actions, which, in turn, lead to our experiencing suffering in cyclic existence.

An alternative translation has

In between meditation sessions, be like a conjuror.

This refers to the period subsequent to the meditation session—how to practice in between meditation sessions—and how even though things are empty, they still appear.

An example of how everything is empty yet still appears is the way our face appears in a mirror. When we see our face in a mirror we know that there's no actual face in the mirror even though there appears to be one there. There's a reflection that exists there and it appears to be a face, but we know that the reflection is empty of being a real face. However, despite the fact that it is empty of real face, at the same time all the various features of a face appear.

The Third Point: Transforming Adverse Circumstances into the Path

THE TEXT NOW RETURNS to the training in conventional bodhicitta.

The general meaning of bodhicitta is the determination to attain enlightenment for the sake of all sentient beings—we want to benefit others in the highest way, we see we have to attain enlightenment in order to do so, and therefore we generate bodhicitta. However, in order to make progress on the path we have to combine our bodhicitta with the realization of emptiness, and when we engage in these profound practices we often encounter hindrances. Therefore we need a method for dealing with them.

By hindrances I mean adverse circumstances or difficult conditions such as getting sick, being in pain or having other things go wrong in ways that harm our mind and stop us practicing. So the discussion of hindrances on the path concerns not only how to prevent them from harming us but also how to transform and use them to enhance our progress.

Insights from this particular explanation on transforming difficult situations into the path are obviously useful for the Buddhist practitioner but even a non-Buddhist can find many ideas here that will be helpful in daily life.

There is a brief explanation followed by an extensive one. The brief explanation is in the next two lines:

When the environment and its inhabitants overflow with unwholesomeness,
Transform adverse circumstances into the path to enlightenment.

When our world is full of pollution and negativity and we, the inhabitants, are also full of negativities and faults, we should transform all this into the path. This means transforming difficult situations into helpful ones, turning hindrances into sources of help, and thinking that those who seem to be harming us are actually helping us achieve enlightenment—seeing them as very kind, as helping us in our practice, particularly that of patience.

Atisha's teacher, Lama Serlingpa, said that difficult situations encourage us to practice because they trigger thoughts of virtue within us and provide us with the best conditions for practicing it.

For example, if we discover that we have a terminal illness and have only two or three more years to live it can encourage us to do better in the short time that we have left. It can make us kinder, more generous and friendlier to our parents and family and people in general—in other words, make us practice Dharma that much more.

Thus, when things go badly for us in any way, through the practice of transforming adverse circumstances into the path we can view any misfortune as a kind of miracle, like a gift from the Buddha to help us in our practice, or as broom sweeping away our negative karma.

Sometimes when people get sick they ask a lama for a divination to see what practices they should do and then they do them. In other words, their illness gets them to practice. It's also said that suffering is a way of waking us up to reality—for example, sickness, pain or any other kind of suffering brings home to us that we are living in the first noble truth, true suffering.

The second noble truth is the true origin of suffering; suffering comes from its true cause—afflictive thoughts and emotions and karma; specifically, suffering comes from the karma we create under the control of afflictive thoughts and emotions. The root of all these afflictions is the self-grasping mind, which is fundamentally mistaken with respect to its objects. It is completely wrong because the way it apprehends things to exist is the complete opposite of their reality. It apprehends objects to exist truly; the actual reality is that everything is completely empty of true existence. In this way our suffering encourages us to reflect on and develop insight into reality.

It is also helpful to think that whatever suffering we're experiencing is the result of karma we have created in the past—in a previous life, perhaps—and that that karma is ripening here, right now. It had to ripen at some time but if it had ripened in a future life it might have made things more difficult for us. For example, at the moment we have the means—money, doctors, medicine and so forth—for dealing with any illness from which we suffer; in future lives that may not be the case, so we should be happy to experience it now, under these favorable conditions.

Moreover, it's helpful to recognize that when we're experiencing suffering we're purifying our negative karma because once that result has ripened we won't have to experience it again.

And the best part is that this is how things actually work. We're not just playing a trick on our mind, distracting ourselves from what's really happening. On the contrary, it makes sense—if we're experiencing suffering we must have created its cause and will eventually have to experience the result. Therefore it's completely valid to think that any suffering we're experiencing is the result of causes we created ourselves.

When we engage in purifying practices such as circumambulation, offering, prostration or meditation we should not think that by doing so we're going to avoid every little problem in this life. However, we *should* understand that these practices will help us to purify much of our negative karma—just not all of it.

For example, it's extremely important to meditate on love and compassion because doing so, even briefly, is a very powerful way of purifying our negative karma. But even though this is true, we can't expect it to stop every little problem. On the contrary, we should *expect* to experience suffering in this life and understand that when we do we're purifying negative karma. In other words, we purify negative karma by doing certain practices and also by experiencing suffering.

Therefore, for the above reasons, it's good to be ill. But it's also good not to be ill, because when we're well we're happy and have lots of energy for practice. This is particularly important at the moment, while we have this precious human life with all its potential; when we're well we have the energy to fully exploit it. When we're healthy there's little we cannot do. We can do all the physical practices, such as prostration, verbal practices, such as mantra recitation, and mental practices, such as meditation on love and compassion. There's essentially nothing we can't do when we're well.

Another thing that can discourage us is being poor but the commen-

tary says that poverty should be a source of happiness. The way to realize this is to reflect on the many difficulties that rich people experience
in working hard to accumulate their wealth; worrying about protecting,
investing, increasing and profiting from it; and being concerned about
its being stolen, losing value, diminishing and so forth. Poor people have
none of these problems.

If we look closely at all the fights and arguments we see around us
we'll find that they're often over money; sometimes we see big fights
over little money. Money can cause many problems.

However, if we're wealthy, we should be happy about that too. From
the Dharma point of view there's no problem in being rich because we
can then make all the offerings we want—or go wherever we want on
vacation! So we should also be happy to be wealthy because of the many
options it gives us. We can give money to the poor, donate it to schools,
hospitals, poor countries and so forth.

However, the best way to use wealth is to accumulate merit because
merit allows us to achieve anything. All happiness, whether short
term—such as that we experience from time to time in this life—or
long term—liberation and enlightenment—results from merit. Once
we've created enough merit, there's no happiness we can't experience.
Wealth is useful because it allows us to create such merit.

The commentary then says that when we approach the time of death,
instead of shaking with fear, worrying and feeling very unhappy about
having to die, we should feel, "It's OK to die now because I haven't created any extreme negative actions, such as the five immediate negativities or the ten non-virtuous actions in a heavy way. I haven't done
anything too bad, so it's OK to die."

Thinking like this at the time of death gives us a better chance of following a path created by merit and being reborn where we can again meet a qualified master who teaches the path to enlightenment and in that way continue following the path.

Of course, if we're ill it's better to regain our health so that we can keep on practicing and strengthening and nourishing the imprints we've already created during this life. Just as seeds gradually develop when we keep adding water and nutrients to the soil in which they're planted and will stop growing if we don't, similarly we need to keep nurturing our karmic potential. Doing so gives us a better chance of getting the results we seek from our practice not to mention a good rebirth.

On top of all that, when we experience difficulties, suffering, pain and the like, we should recall the verse in the *Guru Puja* that says,

I seek your blessings that all karmic debts, obstacles and sufferings
   of mother beings
May without exception ripen upon me right now,
And that I may give my happiness and virtue to others
And, thereby, invest all beings in bliss.[23]

I mentioned before how it can be helpful to think that when something bad happens it's the result of karma, that this is a good way of keeping our mind happy and allowing us to cope when things go wrong. We need to understand that we cannot have everything go the way we want

[23] *Lama Chöpa*, verse 95. This verse is so important that it is recited three times.

just because we want it or stop unpleasant things from happening just because we don't want them to. Things don't happen the way we want. Rather, they happen according to our karma.

Furthermore, when we do face misfortune and think how this is the result of our karma we should also remember that other sentient beings similarly experience a great deal of suffering and use that recollection to inspire us to meditate on compassion. We should also think how much *more* suffering others are experiencing than we are.

The next part is about transforming our attitude through bodhicitta in order to purify our mind and accumulate merit. The root text says,

Apply meditation at every opportunity.

This means that in all situations and locations, whether we're experiencing happiness or unhappiness, we should bring that experience into our meditation and not allow it to distract us from the meditation we're doing.

When things are going well and we're feeling happy we should think, "May all beings be happy and may I be able to benefit them and bring them happiness"; when we're experiencing problems we should think, "Through my experiencing this problem, may no sentient being ever have to experience a single problem again. May I experience all beings' suffering and as a result may the ocean of samsara dry up and completely empty of sentient beings!"

As well as this we can also think that any happiness or suffering we're experiencing is a teaching from our guru on how to practice.

Whenever people criticize us, even without reason, we should think how useful it is because it subdues our mind and prevents us from getting arrogant. Moreover, it helps us identify our faults. If nobody were to ever point them out to us we'd continue to think that we were perfect. When somebody points out our faults it encourages us to rectify them.

We should also be careful when things are going well—we're making money, our relationships are working out, life is good—because at such times we're in danger of our delusions causing us to do things that we should not.

Next, the commentary says that suffering is the path to happiness, which we can relate to the Buddha's teaching on the four noble truths— suffering, the origin of suffering, the cessation of suffering and the path to the cessation of suffering. What this means is that the experience of suffering can make us investigate its nature, see where it comes from, realize it can be ended and follow the path to its cessation and everlasting happiness.

The idea that happiness is an obstacle to spiritual progress and suffering is useful may be found in the small, middle and great scopes of the lam-rim and is also found here in the mind training teachings.

On the small scope we reflect that the usual happiness we experience is not genuine happiness but simply the appearance of happiness. When one type of suffering diminishes we have the impression, or mental appearance, of happiness, but it is not actual happiness, merely a reduction of one manifestation of suffering. By thinking about this, we gradually begin to practice refuge and so forth.

On the middle scope we recognize that even were we to achieve the aim of the small scope—rebirth as a human or a god—the happiness we'd experience would also not be satisfactory or reliable because sooner or later it would come to an end. By thinking about this, we gradually work towards the happiness that completely transcends cyclic existence.

The commentary then explains how on the great scope, for the sake of others, we willingly practice taking their suffering onto ourselves. It also says that if we don't renounce our own personal happiness we'll never be able to generate the mind dedicated to the benefit of others and if we can't willingly accept difficulties we'll never complete the practice of the six perfections.

The supreme method is accompanied by the four practices.

These four practices are:

(a) Accumulating merit in order to achieve enlightenment for the sake of all sentient beings;

(b) Purifying the negativities that hinder our practicing the path;

(c) Offering tormas to spirits and other harmful beings by thinking of their kindness and feeling compassion for them; and

(d) Requesting the Dharma protectors to provide conditions conducive for our mind training practice to improve.

6

The Fourth Point: The Integrated Practice of a Single Lifetime

In brief, the essence of the instruction is
To train in the five powers.
The five powers themselves are the Great Vehicle's
Precept on the transference of consciousness.
Cultivate these paths of practice.

THE FOURTH OF THE SEVEN POINTS is a method of combining all the points into a lifetime's practice, meaning that all the above explanations can be condensed into the practice of the five powers:[24]

(a) *The power of determination*—we must be determined to prevent our mind from falling under the control of self-grasping and self-cherishing.

(b) *The power of familiarity*—the ability to prevent our mind from straying from the mind training practices and to sustain them continuously rather than postponing them until problems

---

[24] *Liberation in the Palm of Your Hand*, pp. 612–16, explains the five powers both as a lifetime's practice and at the time of death as part of Pabongka Rinpoche's explanation of the *Seven-Point Mind Training*.

arise. As is the case in many areas of our life, if we don't rehearse or prepare ourselves ahead of time we find it difficult to succeed in what we do or to deal with problems when they arise. If we familiarize ourselves with the mind training practices from now on we'll find it much easier to employ them when problems actually arise.

(c) *The power of the white seed*—practicing as much as we can to accumulate all the causes we need to succeed in the meditation on equalizing and exchanging self and others.

(d) *The power of repudiation*—thinking deeply about the faults of self-cherishing and self-grasping and rejecting and distancing ourselves from those minds.

(e) *The power of prayer*—dedicating and praying for our bodhicitta to never degenerate but continually increase because of the merit we have created.

There is another set of five powers connected with the practice of the transference of consciousness, as the root text mentions. While the five detailed above relate to practices we have to develop during our lifetime, the other set explains how to think and practice at the time of death. They have the same names but their order is a little different.[25]

With respect to the five powers at the time of death, the power of familiarity includes the position we should adopt when we die—we should lie on our right side with our face resting on our right hand, as

[25] See Lama Zopa Rinpoche's *Death & Dying*, FPMT Inc., 2003; p. 25 (where Rinpoche actually gives both sets in the same order). See also Rinpoche's teaching on the five powers on www.LamaYeshe.com.

the Buddha did when he passed away. It is said that if we do so we cannot be reborn in the lower realms and that this is a method of transferring our consciousness into the upper, or fortunate, realms of rebirth. Therefore the five powers are said to be the Mahayana practice of mind transference. It is also said that we cannot be reborn in the lower realms if we die thinking about and generating faith in the qualities of the enlightened beings.

7

The Fifth Point: The Measure of
Having Trained the Mind

THE FIFTH POINT is the measure, or criterion, of success in the mind training practice. The text says,

Integrate all the teachings into one thought.

We should understand that the one underlying purpose behind all the teachings of the buddhas and bodhisattvas is the elimination of the self-cherishing and self-grasping minds.

Primary importance should be given to the two witnesses.

This means that if, for example, we're falsely accused of stealing, even though we might be able to call up a witness to testify to our innocence, we ourselves are the main witness because we know that we are, in fact, innocent and will not have to experience the karmic results of this action that we have not actually created.

Constantly cultivate only a peaceful mind.

We must sustain our practice whether things are going badly or well. When they go badly we sustain ourselves by using the techniques of transforming difficulties into the path, and, in this way, whatever happens, always maintain our practice and remain on the spiritual path.

Some people tend to get angry at the slightest provocation and say or do all kinds of destructive things. We should not be like that but try to remain steady in our practice. Instead of being touchy and easily upset, when things go badly we should think that it's OK; we should be easygoing. Equally, when things go well, we should think that that's OK too and be easygoing at such times as well. Everybody appreciates easygoing people and their consistency throughout the day. This is how we should be in our practice.

The measure of a trained mind is that it has turned away.

At this point the commentary mentions certain signs indicating some success in our mind training. For example, when we've been practicing for a while, even though we might not have fully abandoned every last sign of selfishness, having been able to weaken it a little is a sign of success. In other words, we know that we're doing well if our selfishness has at least diminished.

There are five great marks of a trained mind.

A person who has practiced mind training may exhibit five great signs:

(a) *The great ascetic*—when we're well trained we can accept all kinds of suffering if doing so enables us to benefit others and sustain our practice and can tolerate difficulties for the benefit of all beings or even just the community in which we live. It has various levels.

(b) *The great being*—we care more for others than ourselves.

(c) *The great practitioner*—our mental, verbal and physical activities mostly, though not completely, accord with mind training.

(d) *The great disciplined one*—we refrain from activities that harm others.

(e) *The great yogi [or yogini]*—we can combine the understanding of emptiness with our activities on various levels for the benefit of others.

By persevering in our practice of mind training we'll find that these five signs gradually manifest and then become stronger and stronger.

The trained (mind) retains control even when distracted.

The commentary says that when we have trained our mind we can maintain control and continue practicing even when we're distracted, just like an experienced horse rider doesn't fall off, even when distracted.

8

The Sixth Point: The Commitments of Mind Training

NEXT ARE THE EIGHTEEN *samayas,* or commitments, of mind training, which teach us to act in ways that are consistent with the mind training instructions.

1. *Don't go against the mind training you promised to observe,*

2. *Don't be reckless in your practice,*

3. *Don't be partial, always train in the three general points,*

We should guard against thinking highly of ourselves just because we're doing this practice for the sake of others and be unbiased in how we relate to all beings—not friendly to some and less friendly to others but friendly and helpful to all.[26]

4. *Transform your attitude but maintain your natural behavior,*

We should change our mind from selfishness to altruism but at the

---

[26] The three general points are these first three commitments. Geshe Tegchok addresses the first and third. Pabongka Rinpoche says that the second means not to use mind training as a pretext for not refraining from harming others by cutting down trees and so forth, pretending to have no more self-cherishing (*Liberation,* pp. 618–19).

same time avoid any external display of having done so. Rather than trying to create the impression that we have changed—like making our eyes look very compassionate to make people think that's how we are— we should just behave normally.

5. Don't speak of others' incomplete qualities,

When somebody has a fault we should not broadcast it to everybody.

6. Don't concern yourself with others' business,

We should not be preoccupied with investigating other people's faults as this is not our business.

7. Train to counter whichever disturbing emotion is greatest,

We should deal with our most evident—that is, most powerful—delusion first.

8. Give up every hope of reward,

When we work for the benefit of others it should truly be in order to attain enlightenment for their sake rather than our own.

9. Avoid poisonous food,

We should not practice mind training just to overcome spirits and so forth or to compete with others in realizations, which would merely perpetuate our delusions instead of destroying them by means of the antidote.

10. Don't maintain misplaced loyalty,

We should not harbor a grudge against somebody who has harmed us in some way by nurturing a grudge and waiting to get revenge. This is similar to the twelfth commitment.

11. Don't make sarcastic remarks,

We should not interfere when others are trying to achieve a virtuous goal or prevent them from doing something positive.

12. Don't lie in ambush,

We should not lie in wait for an opportunity to get revenge on somebody who has harmed us.

13. Don't strike at the vital point,

We should not undermine people in public or recite mantras to overcome spirits, gods and so forth.

4. Don't burden an ox with the load of a dzo,[27]

We should not try to cover up our own mistakes by making out that they are somebody else's, blaming others for errors that are actually our own.

15. Don't abuse the practice,

When working with other people, for example, collaborating on a project, we should not take all the credit, suggesting that although the others helped a bit, we ourselves did most of the work.

16. Don't sprint to win the race,

We should not use mind training simply to overcome those harming us, for example, spirits, or to benefit just our family and friends.

17. Don't turn gods into devils,

If through the mind training practice we become tricky, deceitful or proud, these are examples of turning a god into a devil. A god is supposed to be good but we turn it into a devil; we turn something good into something bad. We should not do this.

18. Don't seek others' misery as a means to happiness.

---

[27] A *dzo* is a cross between a yak and a cow and stronger than an ox.

We should not give others a hard time or cause them to suffer just to find happiness for ourselves. We should not hope to gain happiness through the suffering of others in any way.

9

The Seventh Point: The Precepts of Mind Training

THERE ARE TWENTY-TWO INSTRUCTIONS, or pieces of advice, on mind training.

1. *Every yoga should be performed as one,*

We should combine everything we do—coming, going, sitting, sleeping, eating and all other activities—with the practices of mind training.

2. *All errors are to be amended by one means,*

We should maintain our mind training practice no matter whether things are going badly or well.

3. *There are two activities—at beginning and end,*

When we start any activity, we should generate a positive motivation, especially bodhicitta. When we finish, we should dedicate the merit.

4. *Whichever occurs, be patient with both,*

We should practice patience whether things go badly or well.

5. Guard both at the cost of your life,

We should hold on to Dharma instructions in general and those of mind training in particular, even at the cost of our life.

6. Train in the three difficulties,

The first difficulty is remembering and being mindful of the antidote to a particular afflictive emotion; the second is stopping an afflictive emotion when it begins to arise; and the third is completely severing that afflictive emotion for all time.

7. Seek for the three principal causes,

The first principal cause is to meet a good spiritual teacher; the second is to make the mind suitable, or serviceable, for practice—to put it into good shape; and the third is to eat and drink the right amount, neither too much nor too little.

8. Don't let three factors weaken,

We should not let weaken our faith in and appreciation of our teacher, our delight in mind training, or our conscientiousness in activities of body, speech and mind.

9. Never be parted from the three possessions,

There are three things we should possess by becoming inseparable from them. Physically, we should make prostrations, circumambulate holy objects and so forth; verbally, make requests, recite mantras and so forth; and mentally, never separate from bodhicitta.

10. Train consistently without partiality,

We should practice equanimity and impartiality with all beings and not just be pleasant to our friends, unpleasant to our enemies and ignore or forget those who are neither friend nor enemy. We should be impartial to all.

We might wonder how to do this because friends help, enemies harm and others do neither, but that's only because we're looking at just this one present life. If we take into consideration our countless past lives' experiences, there's every reason to be impartial.

11. Value an encompassing and far-reaching practice,

We should maintain our practice of mind training at all times, in all situations and places.

"Encompassing and far-reaching" means that instead of our mind training being just words we should practice it from the heart.

12. Train consistently to deal with difficult situations,

"Closely related" [28] is the translation of a Tibetan term that has the connotation of "the few singled out from the many." Who do we single out? First, our relatives and friends; second, our enemies; third, those whom we have helped a great deal in this life but have harmed us in response; fourth, those for whom we feel an instinctive dislike because of some particular personal connection, even though they have done us no identifiable harm; and fifth, our parents. It is said to be more difficult to train with these five; therefore they are singled out for special attention.

Let us look at the first of the five—literally, "people at home"; primarily, our partner. Since we have to spend so much time with this person there's a specific risk that things might get fractious. Couples easily get upset with each other, which can lead to all sorts of problems. For instance, one of them has a hard time at work and comes home and takes it out on the other because there's nobody else to take it out on. If this happens we should not immediately get upset and complain, "I haven't done anything. What are you picking on me for?" thereby allowing it to develop into an argument. Instead, we should think that our partner must have had a bad day and is somebody I normally care about and who cares about and helps me so much, and simply let it be, remembering mainly the positive things in the relationship. Let things be and don't let them get out of hand.

With our enemies and those who have harmed us in response to our help, we should practice patience.

With those for whom we feel an instinctive dislike just by seeing them

---

[28] Geshe Chekawa's version of the root text in *Advice from a Spiritual Friend* has "Always meditate on those closely related" as the twelfth precept, which is presumably where this comment comes from.

even though they seem not to have harmed us, we should reflect very carefully on the situation and recognize it as just a karmic obstacle.

Sometimes our parents might scold or nag us. Instead of getting angry we should try to remember that they have always cared for us and been very kind. Even when the children have grown up and the parents are quite old, they still worry about what happens to their kids. We should think that their scolding and nagging is simply a reflection of how much they care for us and not get annoyed or upset with them.

13. Don't rely on other conditions,

We should be particularly careful when things are going well because such times are very dangerous. If, for example, we have no worries about food, clothing, housing and so forth, our mind can get too relaxed, then distracted, and finally let go of the mind training practice altogether. We should be especially vigilant at such times.

We should also be very careful when things are going badly and we're facing many difficulties because again we're in danger of letting our mind training practice go.

It can be quite difficult to practice every single aspect of mind training so we should try to understand the main points in general and train in those. Then, when challenging circumstances arise, because of our familiarity with the main points of the practice, we'll more easily be able to recollect and engage in them.

14. Engage in the principal practices right now,

This means that our future lives are more important than this one and that from looking at our present mind we can get a general sense of what kind of future life we're headed for. Through persistently moving our mind in a positive direction by generating positive thoughts and so forth we can be fairly confident of a good future life. If, however, our mind tends to be more negative than positive, we can be fairly certain of an unfortunate rebirth. This can come about if, through ignorance or apathy, for example, we neglect to practice mind training and as a result our mind is constantly full of negative thoughts and moving in a negative direction.

In general, we should put all the Buddha's teachings into practice, but the mind training ones contain the collected essence of the key points. In this context we can figure out what our most important personal issues are and therefore which practices we should concentrate on.

15. Don't apply a wrong understanding,

There are six kinds of thing we do out of wrong understanding.

The first two are *wrong enthusiasm and patience*, whereby we neglect our Dharma practice and meditation in favor of worldly activities such as drinking, smoking and so forth and allow ourselves to do so.

The third is *wrong compassion*, which means that instead of feeling compassion for worldly people, who are constantly creating non-virtue and the causes for tremendous suffering, we feel compassion for Dharma practitioners, who are working hard meditating, studying and so forth and therefore wearing ragged clothing and not getting much sleep.

Once there was an old lama who looked terrible because of his meager diet. Whenever he went to Lhasa people would feel sorry for him because he looked so pitiful and poor, but he found this quite strange and would tell them, "Well, actually, I feel sorry for you and the way you live."

The fourth is *wrong interest*, which refers to things like monks getting their students—or parents their children—interested in worldly, negative activities instead of spiritual pursuits and Dharma practice.

The fifth is *wrong aspiration*, which means aspiring to worthless, worldly aims and actions instead of positive ones.

The sixth is *wrong rejoicing*, which means rejoicing in others' negative actions instead of virtue and good deeds; for example, thinking of a famous person who has killed thousands of people, "Oh, he was really brave!"

16. Don't be sporadic,

Instead of working hard at our practice for a short period and then giving it up for days, weeks or months at a time because we feel tired or fed up, we should be moderate in everything we do. Moderation in practice means pacing ourselves and practicing at a sustainable intensity. This also entails getting enough food, drink and sleep, all of which are necessary to sustain our body in support of our practice. This is much better than working very hard for a while and then completely giving up. Try to keep going. Some days we might be too busy to do very much, but when this happens we should not give up completely but let go a little, temporarily, and then continue steadily into the future.

17. Practice unflinchingly,

The point here is that the intelligent way to practice is to first think deeply about the teachings to make sure that they're really going to bring the results they promise. For example, we're encouraged to give up the selfish mind, practice altruism and work for the sake of others, so we should investigate carefully to see whether or not it's true that if we do that we'll benefit.

If we examine the teachings like this we will, in fact, find that by practicing in this way our self-cherishing will gradually diminish, our altruism gradually increase and we'll eventually attain enlightenment. Moreover, it is said that when we attain enlightenment our own and others' welfare are achieved simultaneously. Thus by practicing Dharma we will definitely get the results we seek.

Because we're sentient beings, working for the sake of all beings also benefits us; when we accomplish something that benefits all living beings we'll benefit too, just as when we do something for an entire nation we also benefit because we're a part of that population. Through the skillful methods of Dharma, bodhisattvas achieve their own and others' welfare simultaneously. They understand that through completely dedicating themselves to others' welfare their own is taken care of by the way. Thus, when we generate bodhicitta, the determination to attain enlightenment for the sake of all sentient beings, the purpose of others includes our own.

18. Release investigation and analysis,

Here, investigation means checking on a general level and analysis means checking in finer detail. Through checking in both ways we liberate ourselves from problems.

19. Don't be boastful,

We should not show off when working for the benefit of others. When we generate bodhicitta we make a commitment to benefit others, so when we then do something that does benefit them we're simply fulfilling our commitment, which is nothing to boast about.

20. Don't be short-tempered,

We should not make a big fuss when somebody harms us in some small way.

21. Don't make a short-lived attempt,

We should not be over-sensitive, getting euphoric when things go well or depressed when even small things go badly. Instead of always being up and down we should be steady, whether we're dealing with our family, our partner, our workmates or anybody else with whom we're in regular contact. Our emotions should not come and go like clouds in the sky.

22. Don't expect gratitude.

We should not think how good it would be if people knew that we were practitioners in order to get their admiration and respect. Instead, we should keep our practice private. It's OK if people happen to find out but we should avoid really wanting them to know about it.

When the Kadampa lamas of the past neared death they would say that they had spent their whole life practicing according to their teachers' instructions as well as they could and that it was OK that the time of death had come. We too should try to practice like this.

··· 10 ···
Conclusion

THE COMMENTARY I have been following talks about the old and new translation schools. The former means the Nyingma School. Of the four main traditions of Tibetan Buddhism, the Nyingma is the old Kadam and the Sakya, Kagyu and Gelug are the new Kadam. Within these traditions we find slight differences in the wording of the different versions of the root text of the *Seven-Point Mind Training*. This is not a case of correct or incorrect but simply that over the years certain differences have arisen.

The root text I have been following was compiled by the twentieth century Gelug lama, Pabongka Rinpoche,[29] and the commentary I have used was composed by Chigja Rinpoche at the request of Kungo Palden, his manager, who explained that he found the root text and extant commentaries hard to understand and asked Chigja Rinpoche to compose one he could comprehend.

This now finishes the explanation of the *Seven-Point Mind Training* based on that root text and commentary.

Within the entire *Seven-Point Mind Training*, perhaps the most important point is made under the seventh point in the line

[29] See the appendix of this book.

There are two activities—at beginning and end.

As I mentioned in the teaching, the important activity at the beginning is motivation, so please try to be careful with that. Cultivate the habit of thinking about your motivation first thing in the morning, the way a smoker lights up as soon as he gets out of bed. Once we become familiar with setting our motivation first thing, it goes quite smoothly.

However, we have to continue working on our motivation lest faults creep in. It's not enough to assume that since what we're doing is beneficial for others we can just leave it at that and not think about our motivation any more.

On the other hand, if we continue to think about our motivation all the time, our practice won't be quite right either. What we should do is reflect on our motivation at the beginning, do the practice properly and then conclude it in the right way. If we do all this correctly our practice will be complete.

We should also make a habit of reviewing our day before we go to bed each night, asking ourselves how well we did in actually working for the benefit of others, as we set out to do at the beginning of the day. If we find that we did quite well in working for the benefit of others, we should feel very appreciative of ourselves, rejoice, and make prayers and dedications. If we find that we did not do so well, we should try to feel remorse, regret whatever went wrong and purify it. This is the way to shape our mind.

Thus, in the context of the two important activities, one at the beginning and one at the end, the latter is dedication. Dedication is a specific type of prayer we make when we have something to dedicate. If we do something virtuous we can dedicate it with a special prayer; merely saying the prayer itself does not create any merit to dedicate towards the intended result. However, if we have been careful to start our day with bodhicitta motivation, as above, our actions that day should have produced some merit, so that night we should dedicate it to attaining enlightenment for the sake of all sentient beings.

Practicing Dharma in daily life

Even though we talk about these important activities at beginning and end, the teachings actually say that we don't need to set aside a special time for practice. Rather, we should transform all our daily activities— walking, coming, going, sitting, sleeping, eating, working and everything else we do—into practice. We might find it difficult to do this at first because it's hard to remember to do it all the time but if we make the effort it will get progressively easier.

Take the simple activity of eating, for example. There are many ways to eat in a Dharma way, depending upon the level of our practice. Those who have taken bodhisattva vows can transform eating according to Paramitayana or Vajrayana, but at the basic, less esoteric, level we can think simply that we're offering what we're eating to all the sentient beings that inhabit our body, aspiring in future to satisfy them with the Dharma just as we're presently satisfying them with food. In this way we can transform our action of eating into Dharma.

When we go to bed we can recollect the qualities of the Buddha and our various Dharma practices and in that way go to sleep in a positive frame of mind, thus making the whole time we're asleep virtuous.

Therefore, even though it is good to set time aside to do retreat when the opportunity arises, it is probably more important to try to transform all our activities into Dharma. The methods for doing so exist. I know they're difficult and I don't claim to practice them all myself; if someone were to ask me if I can do all these practices I would reply that I cannot do them all. However, it is excellent to try, and the more effort we put in the easier it becomes.

Another thing I'd like to stress is the importance of keeping our mind steady in the sense of not getting too puffed up because of our accomplishments and knowledge, worldly or spiritual. Either way, it's dangerous and harmful. If we find ourselves becoming arrogant we should look around and recognize there are definitely other people who know more and can explain things better. Whatever we feel proud of knowing, we should remember that others know more and looking up to them can help bring our mind back down.

Alternatively, sometimes we might feel a bit depressed, thinking, "No matter what I try, I'm just no good at anything. I'm no good at worldly things; I'm no good at Dharma practice." But if we look around we'll see that there are others who are worse. Comparing ourselves to them can help bring our mind back up.

We need to apply the mental factor of vigilance to check ourselves all the time to see whether or not what we're doing is worthwhile, whether or not we're really practicing. We don't have to be doing anything visible, reciting mantras or sitting in the meditation posture to be genuinely practicing Dharma. As long as what we're doing is truly beneficial for others there's no reason it's not Dharma. Therefore we must be constantly mindful and aware of what we're doing to make sure that we're always on the right track.

There's a story from Atisha's time in Tibet, where he had many disciples. Once he checked to see who had the higher realizations—
Dromtönpa, the disciple who spent all his time serving Atisha, or
Neljorpa, who spent all his time meditating in retreat. What he found
was that Dromtönpa, who continually waited on him hand and foot,
helping and serving him, had more realizations than Neljorpa. That was
because Dromtönpa was constantly vigilant to ensure that everything
he did was of service to his guru. Since he was able to transform all his
activities of body, speech and mind into Dharma, he became the more
highly realized.

Also, when Tibet's great yogi Milarepa was living up in the mountains, people would come up and make offerings of food and help to
the meditators. He observed that the meditators and those offering food
and help became enlightened simultaneously. Actually, the fact that
they reached enlightenment at the same time is a dependent arising.
Like the story of Dromtönpa and the meditator, this story shows that
those who helped the meditators up in the mountains with a good motivation purified much negativity and accumulated extensive merit.

It is said that the root of all Dharma practice is the mind—our attitude
and way of thinking—and that if our motivation is pure, whatever we do
becomes Dharma, whether it benefits others directly or not. There's a
saying that a person with a good mind lying down sleeping is much better than a person with a bad mind sitting in meditation. This is very
true. So what if a person full of malicious thoughts, who always harms
and speaks very spitefully to others, sits up straight, eyes half-closed in
the correct meditation posture? That's not particularly amazing.

What's more remarkable is an ordinary person full of friendly and caring thoughts, who always avoids harming others and is very humble and considerate, lying down to sleep—that person's mind doesn't become negative but continues to grow more positive, even when asleep.

As I mentioned before, when we see that death is imminent we should be able to think, "Well, it's OK to die. I've led my life as best I could, I've not done anything really bad, so there's no reason to regret dying." However, when we see that our death is *not* imminent we should feel happy that we're not about to die and that there are many good things we can do with the rest of our life.

A final note on motivation

Because it is a Mahayana practice, we should never engage in mind training for ourselves alone but always for the sake of all the countless other sentient beings.

When our motivation is to attain personal liberation for ourselves alone, although in general this is neither bad nor non-virtuous because it leads to the state of a Hinayana arhat, it's not appropriate for Mahayana practitioners.

Similarly, if our motivation is to be reborn as a human or a god because we're desperate to avoid the unbearable sufferings of the lower realms, this isn't bad or non-virtuous either—it's still Dharma—but it's a small scope practice and again not worthy of a great scope practitioner.

However, if we practice simply to receive praise, veneration or offerings, gain followers or become rich and famous, then even if we meditate all night and day, it can never become Dharma. No matter how hard we practice, if we're doing it for just this life, it's not Dharma.

For our actions to become Dharma they must be completely unmixed with any thoughts of gain for just this life. If our motivation is mixed with the purpose of this one life, it is deeply polluted and nothing we do will turn out well. It's like pouring nectar into a jar of poison.

The very best thing we can do is to work constantly for the benefit of all sentient beings, who are as infinite as space. If we can't manage that, we should try to gain personal liberation, and if that too is beyond us, then we should at least try to avoid the suffering of the three lower realms. That's still Dharma practice; it's not non-virtue. It's neither wrong nor evil; it's just not the highest practice we can do.

··· Appendix ···
The Seven-Point Mind Training
BY PABONGKA RINPOCHE[30]

Homage to great compassion.
The essence of this nectar of secret instruction
Is transmitted from the master from Sumatra.

Revealing the features of the doctrine to engender respect for the instruction

You should understand the significance of this instruction
As like a diamond, the sun and a medicinal tree.
This time of the five degenerations will then be transformed
Into the path to the fully awakened state.

The actual instruction for guiding the disciple is given in seven points

1. Explaining the preliminaries as a basis for the practice

First, train in the preliminaries.

2. The actual practice, training in the awakening mind
(a) How to train in the ultimate awakening mind
(b) How to train in the conventional awakening mind

[30] From the appendices of *Mind Training like the Rays of the Sun*.

(According to most of the older records, the training in the ultimate
awakening mind is dealt with first. However, according to our own tradition, following the gentle protector Tsong Khapa, as contained in such
works as the *Mind Training like the Rays of the Sun, Ornament for Losang's
Thought, Essential Nectar* and Keutsang's *Root Words,* the order is reversed
for special reasons.)

(a) Training in the conventional awakening mind
    Banish the one to blame for everything,
    Meditate on the great kindness of all beings.
    Practice a combination of giving and taking.
    Giving and taking should be practiced alternately
    And you should begin by taking from yourself.
    These two should be made to ride on the breath.

    Concerning the three objects, three poisons and three virtues,
    The instruction to be followed, in short,
    Is to be mindful of the practice in general,
    By taking these words to heart in all activities.

(a) Training in the ultimate awakening mind
    When stability has been attained, impart the secret teaching:
    Consider all phenomena as like dreams,
    Examine the nature of unborn awareness.
    The remedy itself is released in its own place,
    Place the essence of the path on the nature of the basis of all.

    In the period between sessions, be a creator of illusions.

3. *Transforming adverse circumstances into the path to enlightenment*

When the environment and its inhabitants overflow with unwholesomeness,

Transform adverse circumstances into the path to enlightenment.

Apply meditation immediately at every opportunity.

The supreme method is accompanied by the four practices.

4. *The integrated practice of a single lifetime*

In brief, the essence of the instruction is

To train in the five powers.

The five powers themselves are the Great Vehicle's

Precept on the transference of consciousness.

Cultivate these paths of practice.

5. *The measure of having trained the mind*

Integrate all the teachings into one thought,

Primary importance should be given to the two witnesses,

Constantly cultivate only a peaceful mind.

The measure of a trained mind is that it has turned away,

There are five great marks of a trained mind.

The trained (mind) retains control even when distracted.

6. *The commitments of mind training*

1. Don't go against the mind training you promised to observe,
2. Don't be reckless in your practice,
3. Don't be partial, always train in the three general points,
4. Transform your attitude but maintain your natural behavior,
5. Don't speak of others' incomplete qualities,
6. Don't concern yourself with others' business,
7. Train to counter whichever disturbing emotion is greatest,
8. Give up every hope of reward,

9. Avoid poisonous food,

10. Don't maintain misplaced loyalty,

11. Don't make sarcastic remarks,

12. Don't lie in ambush,

13. Don't strike at the vital point,

14. Don't burden an ox with the load of a *dzo*,

15. Don't abuse the practice,

16. Don't sprint to win the race,

17. Don't turn gods into devils,

18. Don't seek others' misery as a means to happiness.

7. The precepts of mind training

1. Every yoga should be performed as one,

2. All errors are to be amended by one means,

3. There are two activities—at beginning and end,

4. Whichever occurs, be patient with both,

5. Guard both at the cost of your life,

6. Train in the three difficulties,

7. Seek for the three principal causes,

8. Don't let three factors weaken,

9. Never be parted from the three possessions,

10. Train consistently without partiality,

11. Value an encompassing and far-reaching practice,

12. Train consistently to deal with difficult situations,

13. Don't rely on other conditions,

14. Engage in the principal practices right now,

15. Don't apply a wrong understanding,

16. Don't be sporadic,

17. Practice unflinchingly,

18. Release investigation and analysis,

19. Don't be boastful,

20. Don't be short-tempered,

21. Don't make a short-lived attempt,

22. Don't expect gratitude.

This is concluded with a quotation from Geshe Chekawa, who had an experience of the awakening mind:

My manifold aspirations have given rise
To humiliating criticism and suffering,
But, having received instructions for taming the misconception
    of self,
Even if I have to die, I have no regrets.

Colophon

In the literature of the old and new Kadampa there are many versions of the commentaries and root text of the *Seven-Point Mind Training*. The order of presentation and the number of words in them differs greatly. Some of them we cannot confidently incorporate within the outlines when we are giving an explanation, and some include unfamiliar verses in the root text. For these reasons I [Pabongka Rinpoche] had been thinking for a long time of producing a definitive root text by collating the editions to be found in the *Mind Training Like the Rays of the Sun, Ornament for Losang's Thought* and the *Essential Nectar*. When I was teaching the *Stages of the Path to Enlightenment* at Chamdo Jampa Ling in 1935 (wood-pig year), Lamrimpa Phuntsok Palden, a single-minded practitioner, presented me a scarf and an offering and made such a request, so I have compiled this after careful research of many root texts and commentaries and supplemented it with outlines.

··· Bibliography··· and Recommended Reading

Nagarjuna. *Buddhist Advice for Living and Liberation: Nagarjuna's "Precious Garland."* Analyzed, translated and edited by Jeffrey Hopkins. Ithaca: Snow Lion Publications, 1998.

Pabongka Rinpoche. *Liberation in the Palm of Your Hand.* Translated by Michael Richards. Boston: Wisdom Publications, 1991.

Shantideva. *A Guide to the Bodhisattva Way of Life.* Translated by Vesna A. Wallace and B. Alan Wallace. Ithaca: Snow Lion Publications, 1997.

Sopa, Geshe Lhundub. *Peacock in the Poison Grove.* Edited and co-translated by Michael Sweet and Leonard Zwilling. Boston: Wisdom Publications, 2001.

Tegchok, Geshe Jampa. *Transforming Adversity Into Joy And Courage: An Explanation Of The Thirty-Seven Practices Of Bodhisattvas.* Edited by Thubten Chodron. Ithaca: Snow Lion Publications, 1999.

Tsong Khapa, Lama Je. *The Great Treatise on the Stages of the Path to Enlightenment.* Three volumes translated by the Lamrim Chenmo Translation Committee. Ithaca: Snow Lion Publications, 2000, 2002, 2004.

Other teachings on the Seven-Point Mind Training

Chödrön, Pema. *Start Where You Are: A Guide to Compassionate Living.* Boston: Shambhala Publications, 1994.

Druppa, Gyalwa Gendun, the First Dalai Lama. *Training the Mind in the Great Way.* Translated by Glenn H. Mullin. Ithaca: Snow Lion Publications, 1993.

Gehlek Rimpoche. *Lojong: Training of the Mind in Seven Points* (edited transcript). Ann Arbor: Jewel Heart Publications. See www.jewelheart.org.

Gomo Tulku. *Becoming a Child of the Buddhas: A Simple Clarification of the Root Verses of Seven Point Mind Training.* Translated and edited by Joan Nicell. Boston: Wisdom Publications, 1998.

Gyalchok, Shönu & Könchok Gyaltsen (compilers). *Mind Training: The Great Collection.* Translated and edited by Thupten Jinpa. Boston: Wisdom Publications, 2005. (This excellent book contains the root text and several important early commentaries to the *Seven-Point Mind Training* as well as many other essential mind training texts, more than forty in all.)

Gyatso, Tenzin, HH the Dalai Lama. *Awakening the Mind, Lightening the Heart.* San Francisco: HarperSanFrancisco, 1995.

Gyeltsen, Geshe Tsultim. *Mirror of Wisdom: Teachings on Emptiness.* Long Beach and Boston: TDL Archive and Lama Yeshe Wisdom Archive, 2000. (Contains a commentary on the *Mind Training Like the Rays of the Sun.*)

Khyentse Rinpoche, Dilgo. *Enlightened Courage: A Commentary on the Seven Point Mind Training.* Translated by the Padmakara Translation Group. Ithaca: Snow Lion Publications, 1993.

Konchog, Geshe Lama. *Seven Point Mind Training.* On www.LamaYeshe.com.

Kongtrul, Jamgon. *The Great Path of Awakening.* Translated by Ken McLeod. Boston: Shambhala Publications, 1987.

Nam-kha Pel. *Mind Training Like the Rays of the Sun.* Translated by Brian Beresford, edited by Jeremy Russell. Dharamsala: Library of Tibetan Works and Archives, 1992.

Pabongka Rinpoche. *Op cit.* Contains a translation of and a commentary on the *Seven-Point Mind Training*, pp. 589–625.

Rabten, Geshe, and Geshe Dhargyey. *Advice from a Spiritual Friend*. Translated and edited by Brian Beresford, with Gonsar Tulku and Sharpa Tulku. Boston: Wisdom Publications, 1977, 1996.

Tharchin, Sermey Khensur Lobsang. *Achieving Bodhicitta*. Howell: Mahayana Sutra and Tantra Press, 1999.

Trungpa, Chogyam. *Training the Mind and Cultivating Loving Kindness*. Boston: Shambhala Publications, 1993.

Wallace, B. Alan. *Buddhism With an Attitude: The Tibetan Seven-Point Mind-Training*. Ithaca: Snow Lion Publications, 2001.

———. *The Seven-Point Mind Training*. Ithaca: Snow Lion Publications, 1992.

There's also a Web site devoted to this practice:
http://lojongmindtraining.com.

LAMA YESHE WISDOM ARCHIVE

The LAMA YESHE WISDOM ARCHIVE (LYWA) is the collected works of Lama Thubten Yeshe and Lama Thubten Zopa Rinpoche. The Archive was founded in 1996 by Lama Zopa Rinpoche, its spiritual director, to make available in various ways the teachings it contains. Publication of books of edited teachings for free distribution is one of the ways.

Lama Yeshe and Lama Zopa Rinpoche began teaching at Kopan Monastery, Nepal, in 1970. Since then, their teachings have been recorded and transcribed. At present we have more than 10,000 hours of digital audio and some 60,000 pages of raw transcript on our computers. Many recordings, mostly teachings by Lama Zopa Rinpoche, remain to be transcribed, and as Rinpoche continues to teach, the number of recordings in the ARCHIVE increases accordingly. Most of our transcripts have been neither checked nor edited.

Here at the LYWA we are making every effort to organize the transcription of that which has not yet been transcribed, edit that which has not yet been edited, and generally do the many other tasks detailed below. In all this, we need your financial help. Please contact us for more information:

LAMA YESHE WISDOM ARCHIVE
PO Box 356, Weston, MA 02493, USA
Telephone (781) 259-4466; Fax (678) 868-4806
info@LamaYeshe.com
www.LamaYeshe.com

THE ARCHIVE TRUST

The work of the LAMA YESHE WISDOM ARCHIVE falls into two categories: archiving and dissemination.

Archiving requires managing the recordings of teachings by Lama Yeshe and Lama Zopa Rinpoche that have already been collected, collecting recordings of teachings given but not yet sent to the ARCHIVE, and collecting recordings of Lama Zopa's on-going teachings, talks, advice and so forth as he travels the world for the benefit of all. Incoming media are then catalogued and stored safely while being kept accessible for further work.

We organize the transcription of audio, add the transcripts to the already existent database of teachings, manage this database, have transcripts checked, and make transcripts available to editors or others doing research on or practicing these teachings.

Other archiving activities include working with video and photographs of the Lamas and digitizing Archive materials.

Dissemination involves making the Lamas' teachings available through various avenues including books for free distribution, books for sale through Wisdom Publications, lightly edited transcripts, audio CDs, DVDs, articles in *Mandala* and other magazines and on our Web site. Irrespective of the medium we choose, the teachings require a significant amount of work to prepare them for distribution.

This is just a summary of what we do. The ARCHIVE was established with virtually no seed funding and has developed solely through the kindness of many people, some of whom we have mentioned at the front of this book and most of the others on our Web site. We sincerely thank them all.

Our further development similarly depends upon the generosity of those who see the benefit and necessity of this work, and we would be extremely grateful for your help.

The ARCHIVE TRUST has been established to fund the above activities and we hereby appeal to you for your kind support. If you would like to make a contribution to help us with any of the above tasks or to sponsor books for free distribution, please contact us at our Weston address.

The LAMA YESHE WISDOM ARCHIVE is a 501(c)(3) tax-deductible, non-profit corporation dedicated to the welfare of all sentient beings and totally dependent upon your donations for its continued existence.

Thank you so much for your support. You may contribute by mailing a check, bank draft or money order to our Weston address; by making a donation on our secure Web site; by mailing us your credit card number or phoning it in; or by transferring funds directly to our bank—ask us for details.

LAMA YESHE WISDOM ARCHIVE MEMBERSHIP

In order to raise the money we need to employ a fulltime editing team to make available the tens of thousands of pages of unedited transcript mentioned above, we have established a membership plan. Membership costs US$1,000 and its main benefit is that you will be helping make the Lamas' incredible teachings available to a worldwide audience. More direct and tangible benefits to you personally include free Lama Yeshe and Lama Zopa Rinpoche books from the ARCHIVE and Wisdom Publications, a year's subscription to *Mandala*, a year of monthly pujas by the monks and nuns at Kopan Monastery with your personal dedication, and access to an exclusive members-only section of our Web site containing special, unpublished teachings currently unavailable to others. Please see www.LamaYeshe.com for more information.

The Foundation for the Preservation of the Mahayana Tradition

The Foundation for the Preservation of the Mahayana Tradition (FPMT) is an international organization of Buddhist meditation study and retreat centers, both urban and rural, monasteries, publishing houses, healing centers and other related activities founded in 1975 by Lama Thubten Yeshe and Lama Thubten Zopa Rinpoche. At present, there are more than 130 FPMT activities in over thirty countries worldwide.

The FPMT has been established to facilitate the study and practice of Mahayana Buddhism in general and the Tibetan Gelug tradition, founded in the fifteenth century by the great scholar, yogi and saint, Lama Je Tsong Khapa, in particular.

Every two months, the Foundation publishes a wonderful news journal, *Mandala*, from its International Office in the United States of America. To subscribe or view back issues, please go to the *Mandala* Web site, www.mandalamagazine.org, or contact:

FPMT
1632 SE 11th Avenue, Portland OR 97214
Telephone (503) 808-1588; Fax (503) 808-1589
info@fpmt.org • www.fpmt.org

The FPMT Web site also offers teachings by His Holiness the Dalai Lama, Lama Yeshe, Lama Zopa Rinpoche and many other highly respected teachers in the tradition, details about the FPMT's educational programs, audio through FPMT radio, a complete listing of FPMT centers all over the world and in your area, and links to FPMT centers on the Web, where you will find details of their programs, and to other interesting Buddhist and Tibetan home pages.

What to do with Dharma teachings

The Buddhadharma is the true source of happiness for all sentient beings. Books like the one in your hand show you how to put the teachings into practice and integrate them into your life, whereby you get the happiness you seek. Therefore, anything containing Dharma teachings or the names of your teachers is more precious than other material objects and should be treated with respect. To avoid creating the karma of not meeting the Dharma again in future lives, please do not put books (or other holy objects) on the floor or underneath other stuff, step over or sit upon them, or use them for mundane purposes such as propping up wobbly tables. They should be kept in a clean, high place, separate from worldly writings, and wrapped in cloth when being carried around. These are but a few considerations.

Should you need to get rid of Dharma materials, they should not be thrown in the rubbish but burned in a special way. Briefly: do not incinerate such materials with other trash, but alone, and as they burn, recite the mantra OM AH HUM. As the smoke rises, visualize that it pervades all of space, carrying the essence of the Dharma to all sentient beings in the six samsaric realms, purifying their minds, alleviating their suffering, and bringing them all happiness, up to and including enlightenment. Some people might find this practice a bit unusual, but it is given according to tradition. Thank you very much.

Dedication

Through the merit created by preparing, reading, thinking about and sharing this book with others, may all teachers of the Dharma live long and healthy lives, may the Dharma spread throughout the infinite reaches of space, and may all sentient beings quickly attain enlightenment.

In whichever realm, country, area or place this book may be, may there be no war, drought, famine, disease, injury, disharmony or unhappiness, may there be only great prosperity, may everything needed be easily obtained, and may all be guided by only perfectly qualified Dharma teachers, enjoy the happiness of Dharma, have love and compassion for all sentient beings, and only benefit and never harm each other.

· · · · ·

GESHE JAMPA TEGCHOK was born in 1930 and became a monk at the age of eight. He studied the major Buddhist treatises at Sera-je Monastic University in Tibet for fourteen years before fleeing his homeland in 1959 after the abortive uprising of the Tibetans against the Communist Chinese occupation of their country. After staying in the refugee camp at Buxa, India, Geshe Tegchok went to the Central Institute for Higher Tibetan Studies, Varanasi, where he obtained his Acharya (Master) Degree and taught for seven years. He then began teaching in the West—three years in England and ten years at Nalanda Monastery in France, and then in the United States. In 1993, His Holiness the Dalai Lama appointed him as abbot of Sera-je Monastic University in India. He recently retired from that post. Geshela is the author of *Transforming Adversity into Joy and Courage: An Explanation of the Thirty-seven Practices of Bodhisattvas*.

VENERABLE STEVE CARLIER was born in the UK and has been studying Buddhism since the late 1970s, when he first met Lama Yeshe, the founder of the FPMT, and most of his other main teachers. He has been an ordained monk since 1979. Under Khensur Jampa Tegchok's direction, Steve studied at Nalanda Monastery in France from 1982 to 1993, and followed this with eleven years of Geshe studies at Sera Je Monastery in Southern India. Steve has been translating for Khensur Jampa Tegchok since 1989. He has been teaching in the West for many years, sharing his rare experience of living and studying as a Westerner within the traditional Tibetan philosophical system.

ANDY WISTREICH is a member of the Saraswati Buddhist Group in Somerset, England, where he lives with his wife, Shan Tate. Geshe Tegchok was his first Dharma teacher and gave him refuge and precepts in 1980. Andy is the UK Coordinator for Universal Compassion for Wisdom and Peace, and a founding member of the International Kalachakra Network.

LINDA GATTER has received teachings from Lama Yeshe, Lama Zopa Rinpoche and many other great Tibetan lamas since 1978. From 1997–98 she was co-director of Land of Medicine Buddha, California. She began editing books for the LYWA in 1998 and since 2000 has been the Media Manager for Maitreya Project International.

NICHOLAS RIBUSH is director of the LAMA YESHE WISDOM ARCHIVE. A former Australian physician and a student of Tibetan Buddhism since 1972, he co-founded Wisdom Publications with Lama Yeshe in 1975. Over the years he has edited and published many teachings by His Holiness the Dalai Lama, Lama Yeshe, Lama Zopa Rinpoche and other Tibetan lamas.